Praise for

TRUTH ABOUT LOGISTIC!

Deep practical knowledge, yet simple enough for the average person to understand how your food gets from the farmer to your grocery store. A must-read book if you want to have an understanding of food and logistics.
–Jerry Ramirez, Vice President, Business Development, UNIS Fulfillment

For all ages, especially high school students thinking about going into going into the logistics or transportation business as a career.
–Larry Garcia, Educator

This book is a testament to Judy`s passion and dedication to the warehousing and transportation business, and the mechanics that go on behind the scenes to make it all work.
–Tony Almaguer, Vice President, Green Planet 21

Judy is an ACE, the best in the business when it comes to warehousing, transportation and packaging.
–Chris Murphy, Chief Executive Officer, Sierra Pacific Warehouse Group

A must-read book if you want a better understanding of distribution and what it takes to deliver food to distribution centers.
–Matthew "MK" Krause—Regional Logistics Manager, Werner Enterprises

I am thrilled to endorse Truth About Logistics by Judy Jardine. Having had the privilege of working closely with Judy for nearly three decades, I can attest to her unparalleled expertise and deep understanding of the logistics industry. Judy's insights, honed over years of hands-on experience, offer readers an experience-based practical guide to mastering the complexities of logistics. This book is a must-read for anyone looking to gain a true understanding of the field from one of the industry's most respected professionals.
–Mark Hiddleson, Owner, Specialized Storage Solutions

Truth About

Logistics

Truth About

Logistics

One Woman's Thirty-Year Journey in the
Warehousing, Transportation & Packaging World

JUDY JARDINE

Logistics Press

Published by Logistics Press

ISBN (paperback): 979-8-9986271-0-1
ISBN (ebook): 979-8-9986271-1-8

Developmental editing by Ray Anselmo
Book design and production by www.AuthorSuccess.com

Printed in the United States of America

This book is dedicated to my brother John Jardine, the best brother a sister could ever ask for. He was kind, had my back when the chips were down, could fix anything with his hands, was a hilarious practical joker, and could tell stories to all ages and make it believable. (I could tell if he was embellishing or telling the truth.)

Among his other gifts, he was an outstanding gunsmith and an excellent shot who worked with many high-profile gun manufacturers. He also taught gun safety to all ages and even to police departments and academies. He also had an uncanny ability to tell if someone was telling the truth or a lie—the man could read body language like a magazine. And it was all self-taught.

I'm very thankful for the support he and his wife Kathy gave me through my divorce, countless hours talking me through all the drama and how to negotiate the fine details of the settlement. In the end it was the best choice for both of us, since when we got married, we were still children and had not developed the skill set to raise a child and run a household.

John passed away late in 2023 from cancer—he fought a tough fight and God got a good one in Heaven. He left behind Kathy, my lovely niece Julie, and my grandniece and grandnephew Bella and Rocco. I miss him every day, but his legacy will live on—not bad for a boy from the Hayward Hills.

Contents

Author's Note   *xi*

Chapter 1: My First Door Opened and Closed   1

Chapter 2: Mentors from Expected Places   7

Chapter 3: How Marriage Takes a Toll on Work and Vice Versa   11

Chapter 4: For Love of the Warehouse   17

Chapter 5: Who Reads Resumes, Anyway?   21

Chapter 6: The Power of Coupons, Gift Cards   27
           and Friends in High Places

Chapter 7: Union Battles and Other Disappointments   33

Chapter 8: Moving on Up   39

Chapter 9: Work Is Better with Friends: 43

Chapter 10: Have You Heard The One ...?   47

Chapter 11: Abuse and Fallout   55

Chapter 12: Money Owed—No Backing Down   61

Chapter 13: Scandal and Bankruptcy   67

Chapter 14: Safety First   75

Chapter 15: He Died Doing What He Loved   81

Chapter 16: Who Can You Trust?   87

Chapter 17: The "C" Word   95

Chapter 18: Bouncing Back   101

Chapter 19: Holding My Feet to the Fire, Literally,   105
            in Sales School

Chapter 20: Team Play   111

Chapter 21: More than Lipstick on a Pig: Logistics Lessons   115

Chapter 22: Insurance and Other Things to Watch For   127

Chapter 23: Equipment and Other Dangers   131

Chapter 24: Time for a Change   137

If you have ever been the only woman or the first woman in a job, or you have been a pioneer of any kind in some field of endeavor, you know that it can be lonely and scary. You have few people you can ask for advice. There are even fewer people who you can share experiences with.

Work can feel like a hostile place.

As a woman starting out in the 1990s working in a warehouse, I was truly a "first" at almost everything I did. It was complicated by the fact that I was also a single mom raising a young boy. I was told many times to give up on working in a warehouse and that I would regret not going elsewhere. Well, I'm here to tell you I never looked back on that decision, and I have made wonderful friends along the way, many of whom I still have to this day. I not only survived, I thrived. I now have a great job as an executive in logistics, and I also have my own logistics consulting business.

Logistics is a good way to test your survival skills. It has taught me so many life lessons, such as the importance of contracts, how to collect money that is owed to you, what happens when you don't follow customers' instructions, and when to listen to that gut feeling that tells you something is wrong with a situation. That last one has saved my bacon many times.

My hope in sharing these stories is that you will learn from my experiences what is seldom shared about the field. (At a minimum, you will learn how technology makes food magically appear on store shelves.) I want you to be inspired to pursue your dreams and never let anyone take you off your path. And if you are a woman, consider logistics as a career choice. You will never be bored.

Judy Jardine
Modesto, California
August 26, 2024

CHAPTER 1

My First Door Opened and Closed

When I was five, my father, Lee Jardine, decided he wanted to relocate our family from Oakland, California to Hayward, where he had bought some land to raise horses and chickens. He wanted us to plant a garden and raise our own vegetables.

The problem was that there was no house on the land.

He managed to find a home already built in Hayward (where the Southland Mall now sits), sitting in an orchard with a barn. Now he just had to have it moved to the land he'd bought—and that was a task. First a pad had to be cut to sit the house on—the property sat on a hill with only a dirt road leading to the property. Then, since there was no gas or sewer hookup, a septic tank had to be dug and tested for drainage.

The house was moved on railroad ties by a house-moving company. It took over six months to move it to the property during one of the worst winters on record—nonstop rain, and the dirt roads were washed out in many places.

Finally in the spring we were able to move into the house and away from the city to farm life. I even got the pony that I had always wanted, though he had to be staked out—hobbled—until a fence could be built. I could see the stars at night and even see the top of the Golden Gate Bridge from the rooftop ledge outside my bedroom window. It was so quiet at night I could hear the horses talking to each other and the sheep baa-baaing. I was living the dream.

At the time my father worked for Royal Jersey Farms, delivering milk, eggs and butter to homes in Castro Valley and Hayward. The housewives loved his charm and he always made high sales. Plus, we always had fresh milk, eggs and plenty of ice cream. As a child I loved going into the freezer and picking out whatever ice cream I wanted.

However, Dad wanted to make more money and he felt his talent for sales was being wasted. So he enrolled in insurance classes to become an independent insurance broker. That turned out to be his calling, and he soon built a thriving insurance business, Jardine's Independent Insurance Agency on Mission Boulevard in Hayward.

(Interestingly, one of my dad's customers, a general contractor, was the brother of the owner of a warehouse and distribution company. Little did I know that one day I would be working for that company. Small world.)

Dad got involved with the city and soon became the Hayward Fire Marshal. He sat on the Hayward City Council for a time and handled all the insurance on the local school buildings and major construction in the city. I learned a lot about insurance and claims, information that would be invaluable later in my life.

I would join my father at the city council meetings and watch how he worked the room, shaking hands and making coffee dates. He told me never to mix religion and politics and never to gossip about people's personal lives. In private my dad would share all the dirt, underhanded dealings and so on. But never in public.

Growing up in the Hayward Hills on a farm was life-changing, and the skills I learned would serve me well later in my logistics career. We had horses, chickens, and a steer we raised for slaughter to fill our freezer with beef. We planted and grew our own vegetables, corn, and had apple and cherry trees.

I loved riding my horses in gymkhana events as well as barrel racing. With my horse Rawhide, I won many belt buckles, ribbons and even prize money. It was hard work keeping the stalls clean, feeding the horses at 5:00 a.m., long workouts in the arena after school each day to keep my horses in top condition for the events, and keeping my saddle and tack in working order.

I rode in the Grand National at the Cow Palace in South San Francisco, Rowell Ranch in Hayward (I was Rodeo Hostess Queen), the Pendleton Roundup in Oregon and every local rodeo that had barrel racing and gymkhana events. Not only was it great experience, but I loved the thrill of the competition and meeting and greeting the public.

One year the school bus drivers went on strike and we had to ride our horses to school, tying them up at the fence by the football field. All the horse manure all over the place helped end the bus strike quickly.

I was also a 4-H member and had to keep log books on how much I fed my lambs, the cost of fuel to transport them, and overhead costs. I showed my lambs at the Alameda Country Fair and sold them for top dollar to Lucky and Safeway grocery stores. I always took first place—blue ribbons meant more money per pound—and made a profit every year.

4-H showed me how to keep accurate records as I had to be accountable for every penny I spent to get the lambs to market and the stores. I was up every morning at 5:00 a.m. to feed all the livestock before going back up to the house, taking a shower, and walking a mile and a half to the bus stop to catch the bus that took us another six miles to school.

I learned how to fix and mend fences, barbed wire and electrical, repair water pumps, dig post holes for new fence lines—just about everything on a farm that needed to be repaired I had to learn fast. And we didn't have the option of Googling it. My father would instruct me on how to fix and repair most anything, though for some things beyond my capabilities we had to hire an expert.

This was all while Dad was working long hours in his insurance business. I spent my summers working for my father in his insurance office, filing claims and taking payments. I learned a lot about the insurance business. One claim I recall involved the homeowner getting drunk, running his car into his house and trying to claim the car did it on its own.

I enjoyed going out on sales calls with my dad and learned a lot about the community, and the people and relationships as well. It was all about service and asking the right questions. You have to give before you receive—it's important to build and establish relationships, whether with family members or a committee.

As Fire Marshal, Dad did all the hiring and firing of the firefighters and chief. I can remember many times sitting on the sidelines watching him interview cadets and firemen for positions. Most were nervous, and some were prepared while some were not.

One night we awoke to our fence and retaining wall on fire. My dad was burning trash in a 55-gallon drum; the wind came up during the night and blew the hot ashes on the retaining wall. Dad had to call his own fire department and report that the fence was on fire, He tried to keep it out of the newspapers, but it was on the front page the next day. Needless to say, he was embarrassed to be the talk of the town.

Living with two brothers was a real adventure. They were always pranksters, full of nonstop teasing. Since I was the oldest it was my responsibility to take care of them—cooking meals, washing their clothes and making sure they stayed out of trouble. Or trying to make sure they stayed out of trouble. They liked to do things like riding motorcycles on private property or chasing girls. The younger one once got drunk, came home from a high school party, ran his car onto the front lawn and through the front room window of a neighbor's home. That one we managed to keep out of the papers.

My other brother John was hard working, always busy making money and working out. He'd had polio at the age of 18 months and the doctors told us he would never walk again. My father told all the doctors they were wrong, went home and built a small gym in the garage, with weights and an exercise bicycle, for my brother to work out on. He also contacted the Shriners in Oakland, who said they could perform two operations to help John build his leg and calf muscles back. They were experimental operations that included removing part of a bone from his hip and replacing it in his big toe. (Without your big toe, you have no balance, and it's very difficult to walk.)

The operations were successful, and after John healed he started working out again. He'd put up pictures of Arnold Schwarzenegger and other bodybuilding celebrities. He even went down to Laguna Beach and worked out with Arnold several times. He would come back so pumped and I knew he was taking this very seriously. Eventually John started competing in bodybuilding events. He even took fifth place in Mr. Teenage America, which put him on the front page of several bodybuilding magazines.

The most gratifying part was when my father took my brother and me to visit all the doctors who told him he would never walk again. Their jaws dropped in disbelief.

John got a commendation from the mayor of Hayward for his recovery. A year later he built Jardine's Health Spa & Racquetball Club off of Mission Boulevard in Hayward. Later he added a sports bar to the gym that supplied all of the members with protein drinks and healthy foods that they could eat there or take out. He was big on nutrition and supplements, always looking for healthy ways to improve one's body and mind. He also got involved with helping the handicapped with special workout bikes and equipment.

Everyone knew who John Jardine was, and everyone in town had great respect for him. I would work out at my brothers gym four or five times a week, and occasionally work at the front desk taking keys for lockers and helping sign up new members. It was a great place to network too. To this day I still work out and have my own Pilates machine.

Through all the difficulties, my father had to support my mother, me and my two brothers, so where we spent our money had to be budgeted—food, clothing, rent and what have you. But success was in his DNA and he was always positive.

One of the great gifts I learned from my father is to have a vision (written out!), to stay focused every day and never give up. You have to apply yourself to every job and never judge or talk badly about people, especially in business. Kindness goes a long way. He practiced what he preached and that made him very successful in the insurance business. Despite all the competition, he always had high sales and received free trips to Las Vegas, all expenses paid.

The old saying is if you have your health and a sound mind you can accomplish anything in life. My father Lee Jardine instilled that in me at an early age, and it has stuck with me to this day. If you set your mind to it, nothing is impossible.

CHAPTER 2

Mentors from Expected Places

My grandfather Sam Jardine owned the Good Housekeeping Shop in Oakland, selling washing machines, bedroom sets and refrigerators. He was the best salesperson I have ever seen in action—he could sell ice to the Eskimos, as they used to say. It was a real talent in those days when money was tight, but he always found a way to establish credit and payment plans. The customers loved him.

Grandpa Sam was a no-pressure salesman—he'd just give the facts on how a new mattress or washing machine would keep the lady of the house happy. He'd also get the skinny on the whole clan, including all the cousins and extended family. A week later another member of the family would come into my Grandpa's shop and he'd sell them a bedroom set along with a washer and dryer. Networking with every member of the family paid off in the long run in repeat business. It also didn't hurt that Grandpa would give them a 10% discount on the next purchase.

He would also do his own credit deals with 2% interest and no pre-payment penalties. He knew he would be paid back at tax time from all the refunds. He was always prepared to meet people's immediate needs—for instance, if a family had a new baby, he knew that meant they needed new nursery furniture.

He knew logistics well, like knowing when the containers would arrive at the Port of Oakland. He'd make sure that when the containers arrived, he had the manpower to unload them and get everything staged in the showroom, with the back room filled to the rafters with merchandise. I suspect some city codes were broken, but he knew where every piece was stored.

My grandfather loved Cadillacs and bought a new one every year. He would do his gift giving during the holidays in those Cadillacs, his trunk filled with whiskey, brandy, wine, candy, pasta, toys for the children, fresh flowers for the woman of the house and cigars for the men who smoked them. (I loved to tag along on those trips.) He was immaculate in his business attire: double breasted suits and freshly pressed slacks. He always carried breath mints and his fingernails were well manicured. He looked as if he'd just stepped out of *GQ Magazine*.

I would spend Saturdays at the Good Housekeeping Shop with him, watching him work his sales magic. Grandpa only had a seventh-grade grade education, but he taught himself all about people types and sales. He was a perfect example for me of how hard work and application led to success.

Since my grandpa knew everyone in town, I saw how he impacted their lives even if they had very little money. Once, a very young family had their first child and needed a crib and a chest of drawers with a changing table on top. Grandpa knew just what to do—he called up one of his customers and asked them to trade in their old baby furniture set, telling them he would pay them cash along with 10% off a new adult twin bed and dresser. It worked—they came in and bought the new teen bedroom set. Grandpa picked up the used baby set and delivered it to the young couple that same day.

This made such a big impact on me—and the young couple. A few years later the youngsters came back to Grandpa's showroom floor and purchased a new master bedroom set, dining room set, and a washer and dryer.

Grandpa Sam was great businessman who had also known hard times—he never forgot that and always helped his customers any way he could, because he knew they would return the favor and recommend his furniture shop to their family and neighbors. What an inspiration he was. In my eyes he was my hero. Later on in my logistics life, I would use the skills Grandpa showed me to an even greater degree.

He wasn't the only good influence in my family. There was also my father's sister, my Aunt Dorothy. I was lucky to have such an amazing auntie to talk to—she had plenty of confidence and natural common sense, and would give me sound advice without judging me. It didn't hurt that she worked for several high-profile business people in the area and knew how the world worked.

I mentioned that I was very involved in 4-H in my teen years. 4-H taught me a lot about being organized, taking notes, managing my time, and planning ahead for special events like the Alameda County Fair or horse shows at the Cow Palace in San Francisco. I had to keep records on how much I spent on hay, grain, vet bills, shoeing my horse and the like. Getting a horse shoed even back then was pretty pricey, and nowadays it's crazy expensive—like buying a whole new set of tires for your truck or car. Most of the money I made off of raising my lambs and selling them at the county fair helped support my horsemanship activities, plus having extra money left over for myself.

Anyway, once I failed a proficiency test for 4-H and was devastated. I called Aunt Dorothy for guidance and she gave me pointers on how to study and remember the correct answers. The next time I took that test I got a perfect 100% score. I was thrilled and so proud of myself—not to mention motivated to do more reading and learning.

There was also the family of one of my best friends. Her parents "Roger" and "Mary" (not their real names) would let me join them on weekend trips to their cabin on Lake Tulloch near Angels Camp in the Sierra Nevada foothills. We'd go water skiing behind the awesome boat they'd had built just for that activity, and sit around a campfire at night talking about boys and high school and what we wanted to do after we graduated. Some evenings my friend and I would go into town, sneak into bars and have a cold beer (this was before bars were required to check I.D.).

I learned more from Roger about "the facts of life," what boys wanted and how to avoid the pitfalls than I even did from my dad. And his older daughter, my friend's sister, would take us to the mall to shop for cute dresses and high heels. We'd hit the makeup counter for foundation, mascara and nail polish, then go back to their home where her older sister would show us how to put it all on. We'd turn up the music in her bedroom, dance to the music and act crazy, often while practicing walking in high heels.

Those days were fun, and we looked all put together when went back to school on Monday. As I came from a family of all boys, I was kind of a tomboy myself, so those times spent with my friend and her sister were a blessing, learning how to be more feminine.

My younger brother John was also always there to support me and let me know when my mother was on the warpath, which admittedly could be any day ending in a Y. I also mentioned that I was doing a lot of cooking and cleaning for the family—that was because Mom couldn't be relied on to take care of it. Sometimes she'd verge into flat-out madness, triggered by nothing more than an offhand comment or me looking at her "the wrong way." We'll deal with that in depth later.

But between Grandpa, my father, Aunt Dorothy, Roger, Mary and John, I was saved from making a lot of very stupid mistakes. Not that I didn't make some, but thanks to them it wasn't far worse.

CHAPTER 3

How Marriage Takes a Toll on Work and Vice Versa

As soon as I graduated from high school I went job hunting and in the first week I received three job offers. I took the job with Continental Can—it was for the summer only, but it paid the most per hour. At the end of the summer, they asked that I stay on as a full-time employee on the night shift. I said yes and I worked there for another 17 years.

So now I was working, making good money, and I bought a Chevrolet El Camino. It was a fast car with 18-inch rims and low-profile tires—and I loved cruising East 14th Street in San Leandro every Friday and Saturday night with my girlfriends. I got in a little trouble with the boys in that era, doing stupid young-girl stuff like double-booking dates on the same night. Plus just before I graduated from Hayward High I got engaged to my boyfriend because he was leaving for Vietnam. That was a big mistake, and I returned his ring after he came home.

Still, looking back it was all rather tame. A lot of my girlfriends from high school got married young, many of them because they were already pregnant. That was a bullet I dodged, thank Heaven. And I still lived at home, not only paying rent to my parents but also cleaning the house and doing most of the cooking for my brothers and father. I was the only girl and the oldest, so my father put me in charge. If I wanted to go out with my girlfriends, I had to make sure the house was clean and food ready when he arrived home. So I had responsibilities.

But I had my car and was shopping at Macy's every Friday afternoon for a new outfit—I was a bit of a fashion diva. I took a second job part-time at a convalescent hospital just to afford my nice lifestyle.

With two good jobs I was able to go to Lucca's Delicatessen in Castro Valley and order salami, ravioli and all kinds of delicious Italian food. I soon learned not to bring leftovers home, however—I tried to hide them in the back of the refrigerator, but my brothers would find them, eat them all and put the empty containers back.

Even with all those luxuries, I managed to save money and have a good-sized bank account. I could even upgrade my car, to a Corvette that I saw at F.H. Dailey Chevrolet in San Leandro.

In a few months that Corvette was mine and I drove it off the showroom floor and went cruising with my girlfriends. Guys would stop us and tell me to park my boyfriend's car and go cruising with them, but no, this was my car. The looks of shock on their faces when they found out were epic. Don't kid yourself—working my ass off had its benefits.

But saving and working hard would really pay off later after I got married and faced some tough times.

I met my husband on East 14th one summer night while cruising. We fell in love hard and fast, and got married in less than a year. We had a big wedding at All Saints Catholic Church in Hayward with six bridesmaids and a maid of honor, over 200 guests, a band and wonderful food. We honeymooned in Carmel and it was amazing.

We moved into a two-bedroom, one-bath house built in the 1920s—very cute and small. I had fun decorating it, even making new curtains for all the windows. All the money I had saved before we got married bought all the furniture and a secondhand truck for my new hubby. I was the breadwinner, as he'd lost his job with Pacific Gas & Electric the day before we got married. I didn't tell my father about that until years later—if I had, he would have never allowed me to get married.

Even then, he seemed to see what I didn't. The whole time he was walking me down the aisle he kept suggesting we turn around and go back, that I didn't have to marry this guy. He must have asked me fifty times if I really wanted to go through with it. I almost broke down but I held it together.

The first year of marriage was good and we enjoyed being married. Then my husband wanted to buy a boat and I wanted a home with more rooms to decorate and a big yard. We got both and I had my son David, who was a blessing from Heaven.

All was good until my husband started getting promotions at work, making a whole lot more money. He'd started out as an order picker at a firm in Union City, California on swing shift, and only got that job because his brother-in-law worked there. Then his ego got the best of him and he started treating me very badly, verbally abusing me and drinking a lot. He would go out with customers and stay late for meetings and his treatment of me and our son started to escalate pretty fast. He would always remind me how much money he made and that I'd better do as I'm told or he would see to it that David would be taken away from me and no attorney would be able to protect me.

In our ten years of marriage we moved eight times, always to a bigger home, usually along with a bigger boat that we really didn't need. My husband was a free spender—he would say he was going for a six-pack of beer and return home with a new car or truck without ever consulting me.

That wasn't the only problem he caused. Once we attended a party for his company and he told me not to move from the head table if I knew what was good for me. Well, one of the other supervisors asked me to dance with him and I took him up on it. I got a dirty look from my husband that I'd better sit down—he was sitting at the bar the whole time with his secretary. The man I was dancing with told me I'd better open my eyes because my husband was sleeping with that secretary.

While my dearly beloved was buying himself new vehicles, I had an old Chevy Nova that was held together with baling wire and duct tape. (I'd sold the Corvette before we got married so my husband could buy a truck.) My co-workers would ask me "Does your husband love you? Your car is always breaking down." The mechanic at work was always working on my car because my husband would tell me not to have any work done on that car without his permission or else. Every day I was putting water in my radiator just to get to work, then filling it up with water before I could make the ride home. Good thing I was only about ten minutes from work.

Then one day my radiator would not hold any more water so I had it towed to a shop and had it fixed. My husband had a fit and blew up in my face—verbally abusive once again. By now I knew it was over, so I found an attorney and when I told her about all the shit he put me through, she said not to worry.

Around this time my husband bought another house in Tracy, California—again without my consent (he signed my name to all the documents). It was a five-bedroom, three-bath monstrosity with a bonus room for parties and a pool table. That night when he arrived home he told me to quit my job and to get another job in Tracy, and to find a babysitter because we were moving again. As it was, we had to move into my mom's home for a few months until the home was finished.

Then he sprung on me that he was staying in Fremont close to work because he was not a commuter. He would get a small apartment for during the week and only come home on weekends.

Enough was enough. I had him served with divorce papers at work. Talk about shock—he had so many questions about how did I found time to get an attorney and have me served, and where I got the money. Apparently he forgot I still had a job.

That night he said goodbye to David and found a room at a nearby hotel. I was left having to explain it to David, and I know that as young as he was, he didn't understand. A very sad day, but a necessary one.

David and I lived at my mom's home for six months before we got our own place, a cute little apartment we moved into with no furniture. We slept on sleeping bags for the first few months, then shared a futon until I could afford a separate bed for David. We were happy and had fun on short weekend road trips. We had to move many times due to rent going up and a roach infestation that the landlord would never address. Finally we found a very nice townhouse with a washer and dryer—no more trips to the laundromat. We were close to all the stores and they had a security system so we felt safe.

We got $200 a month in child support from my ex, which helped, plus I was still working at Continental Can so I had medical coverage for my son and myself. We were poor but happy, with a whole lot less drama with my ex-husband not being around. (Pete wasted no time—he married his secretary within a year after our divorce.)

I'd like to say things went happily ever after, but real life doesn't work that way. Seven years after my divorce, Continental Can was bought out by Quaker Oats in Chicago. They laid off everyone on a Friday, and I was out of a job for the first time since high school. But better things were to come.

CHAPTER 4

For Love of the Warehouse

So there I was, in my mid-thirties, a single mother raising a son on my own, and I'd just been laid off from my job of seventeen years after the business had been sold. Time for job hunting. So I hit the streets first thing Monday morning.

The fourth business that I applied at was at J&R, a warehouse and distribution center in Hayward. Not only were they hiring, but they told me to go to St. Rose Hospital to take a drug test, and if I passed the drug test to come right back—they had a job for me!

Believe it or not, I started that day and was put right to work entering orders and answering the phones. Can you imagine that happening today?

Three days later I was given a tour of the warehouse. Wow! I had never seen that much food on pallets in my entire life. Forklifts were running back and forth loading and unloading trailers and putting pallets away in the racks. It was at that moment that I fell in love with the warehousing business.

But there was so much to learn. I got educated on lot codes, FIFO (First In, First Out), BBD (Best By Date) and a hundred other acronyms. I was like a sponge soaking up all the inventory information.

People were so helpful and I knew I had found my forever home in the warehousing and third-party logistics (3PL) industry.

Having been raised on a farm and had sheep that we raised for and sold at the fair, I was now seeing the other end of the process: watching the lamb chops go to the big supermarkets. *So this is how the supply chain works,* I thought. For the most part, most people today do not know how their food arrives at the stores, all they know is that they push their shopping cart around and fill it with stuff.

Other things went on behind the scenes that frankly had nothing to do with warehousing. For instance, one day I happened along and the shipping and receiving office door was open—I saw a lot of money on the table in the office. Hmmm, this was different.

Then the shipping and receiving dispatcher walked in and said "What the hell are you doing in here? This is off limits! Better not say a word about what you saw!"

Scared shitless, I said "I know nothing!" (That was true enough—I was so naive then!)

I found out later that nothing sinister was happening. The company had small weekend football pools that involved a handful of warehouse workers and drivers during the season—technically illegal, I suppose, but nothing you couldn't find in almost any office at the time. The other cash, about $3,000, was money they'd give the drivers to reimburse them for unloading at a few of the local supermarkets. They'd only chase out people who weren't involved so they didn't have to worry about someone stealing it. Just another day at the office.

Sometimes there really was some craziness. "Pops" was the father of the current owner, and had been one of five partners in a transportation company based out of Milwaukee that trucked product all over the Midwest. When his sons opened a warehouse in California in the mid-1960s, Pops worked with them, shipping candy, confections and other food commodities from the Midwest to Oakland, California, from which they would deliver to all the local chain stores. The manufacturers sold to those chains nationwide, so it was handy to have an outlet on the West Coast.

Warehouse space in Oakland was a lot cheaper and more space was available to lease than across the Bay in San Francisco. Eventually they acquired two more warehouses just to handle all the customers. By then the company was working with a lot of high-end factories, numerous pasta companies and a load of candy manufacturers.

Pops was a hoot and had his own way of making things happen or lighting a fire under your butt. Once he told me the ink on my check was not going to dry because I had hung up the phone on one of his best friends. It wasn't my fault—there was no place to park the incoming calls. They just got dropped and they would have to call back again. I stood up and told him his system was outdated and he needed to install a new and improved system if he didn't want his friends hung up on.

I proceeded to tell Pops he didn't know what he was talking about and to let me make some calls and get quotes on a new phone system. My supervisor was giving me hand signals to shut up and sit down before I got fired, to stop talking back to Pops and just let it go. I didn't, and Pops said "I want to see you in my office now!"

He didn't fire me, though—he said that if I thought I was so smart, to go ahead and get a new phone system and he'd be the judge. You guessed it—I had a new system installed in ten days for a 60-day free trial at no charge. We'd only keep it if Pops approved. He did, because the office girls loved it and so did the management team. We got a huge upgrade on our phone system, all because I spoke up and I knew what I was talking about.

Funny thing … Pops never yelled at me again, and always called me into his office to discuss any issues he was having. He also asked for advice in a very nice tone of voice. We became good friends.

I don't care what warehouse or 3PL firm you work for, there is always dirt to be found, always some kind of shenanigans going on. As I used to say, "Love, lust and lies are going on somewhere in this operation." There were employees and co-workers trying to cover up affairs all the time, especially if things were not going well at home or in other areas of their lives, including secret rendezvous at lunch or when one of the truck drivers has a sleeper cab in their vehicle.

And the lies they tell you—no, nothing is going on! Until the girl you think is fooling around with your guy comes up pregnant ... hmmm, wonder how that happened? I'd think to myself it was a good thing I never slept with him—just a gut feeling that told me he was no good and to keep moving on.

One all-time rule: never, but NEVER sleep with your boss, especially if you know he's married. I used to keep a flow chart of the names of girls that slept with one particular boss—sure enough, when his wife found out about each hussy, that girl was out of a job!

Once a very good friend of mine was watching another boss hit on me all the time and knew I was at the end of my rope. One day I received this big flower arrangement. Said boss walked by my office, pulled out the card that said "Love you to the Moon and back! XOXO!" and asked me "Why didn't you tell me you had a boyfriend?" I said, "You never asked." That boss never approached me again! A quick fix and no one lost their job.

(I thanked that friend of mine with a $300 bottle of wine, and asked him what took him so long to order the flowers. He said he wanted to make me sweat a little so I would get the lesson. We still laugh about it to this day!)

CHAPTER 5

Who Reads Resumes, Anyway?

Shortly after I started at J&R Distribution, there was an opening for a Value Added Manager to handle all of the packaging business for deliveries to the big membership warehouse stores. They even posted an ad in the local newspaper. What they didn't know, but should have, is that I'd already had that experience at my previous job.

In the meantime, I was looking for a higher-paying position, as I was living paycheck to paycheck at my current job—I'd taken it just to put food on the table. (Single mom, remember?) I had found another job making twice as much money right down the street from where I was.

It was only when I gave my one-week notice that they thought to look at my resume. The next thing I knew, I was being called into the Vice President's office on a Thursday and being questioned why I hadn't said something sooner about my past work experience. My thinking was that it wasn't my fault they hadn't read my resume when I was hired two months before. (Of course at the time I was just glad to be getting any job at all.)

The VP didn't speak for a moment, just sat there thinking. Then he asked me how much money I was going to be making at my new job and I told him—double. More silence. Now the man is really thinking about how to convince me to stay and take on this new role as the Value Added Project manager. He made me an offer I couldn't refuse—he'd match what they were offering and toss in an end-of-the-year bonus based on total profits.

Deal!

"Oh, by the way, you start tomorrow and five people will be reporting to you. And we have our first customer arriving on Monday. You need to be prepared to do a PowerPoint presentation at 9:00 a.m. sharp."

No pressure. Furthermore, I had no background on the customer, other than they were a cookie company, and their product was coming from the UK on container ships across the ocean. But I was still willing to take it on, and I had some samples of their product. I could do a time study to come up with a quote per pack and per case, including storage, handling, shrink wrap, labor, labels, the whole nine yards.

So I work through the weekend, morning, noon and night. I did take a break on Saturday to go to Goodwill and buy a nice secondhand suit so I could look professional on Monday morning. I lucked out with a nice-looking suit jacket and a black pencil skirt for only $32.50, which would have likely cost me $250 easy at Macy's. As it was, raising my son David by myself at the time, money was tight. Even a Goodwill suit meant we'd be eating tacos four nights a week for a while instead of just two. Sometimes you just have to roll the dice and see what happens.

(I still have the jacket to this day—a Donna Karan.)

The meeting starts Monday at 9:00, and we all introduce ourselves, shake hands, give our background and go into our spiel on why the cookie company should be doing business with us and how we provide a superior 3PL service to our competitors. The PowerPoint starts and everything is going great. At the end I give a written quote to provide all of their logistics and packaging services.

The cookie company representative came unhinged! First he says my packaging price is too damn high and he would never do business with us. Then he proceeds to tell me I need to go home and make babies because I clearly don't know what I'm doing.

I managed to hold it together until I walked out the lobby doors. Mercifully, my boss had my back and told me the cookie company guy was a real piece of work and to stand my ground. Still, not a great second day in the new position.

I went home, had a good cry and spent time with David, thinking to myself that I did a damn good job on my presentation and my pricing was spot-on. Besides, the cookie people were not going to find another 3PL company to do everything under one roof including packaging—no one else in the area had the capabilities.

Back at the office, we were working six days a week, providing packaging and other services for a bundle of major conglomerates. I had a great team and we worked together as a family—literally! I know that's a cliche in the business world, but we actually spent birthdays, family gatherings, weddings and so much more together. The sun wasn't going to rise and set on one British biscuit baker.

Then this call comes through to my boss. The person on the other end says he's so-and-so from the cookie company and he wants to accept our offer on the warehousing and packaging business! My boss, bless his heart, tells him you're talking to the wrong person—you need to be talking to Judy Jardine. He puts him on hold, runs into my office and says that piece of work from the cookie company is on the line and wants to sign a contract accepting our pricing. He also tells me to make him wait because he only wants to talk a man, not a woman. (Tee hee!)

Well, I can follow my boss' orders. After making him wait a good long time, I pick up the phone and say, "Hi, this is Judy Jardine, how can I help you?"

I can tell he is nervous about having to talk to me. He tells me he wants to move forward with the contract and he will sign it right away. I tell him that the pricing was from last month and that I will need to revisit the pricing and get back to him. He's now in a full-blown panic—turns out he has two containers on the water at that very moment, due to arrive next week, and he has a purchase order from one of the huge warehouse store chains that needs to be filled three days after we receive the product! If we don't help him out, he may not get another P.O. from the store chain and could lose their business altogether.

It was so tempting to tell him I was sorry, I couldn't help him because I was going home to make babies. Instead, I was professional, and we signed the contract that day. Further, we received and unloaded the containers, packaged the cookies and made the ship date to the store chain's distribution center on time. I really owed it to the team because we had to pull some strings to get the appointment date and make it happen there, and we worked over the weekend to complete the packaging of the 3-paks just in the nick of time.

That fellow at the cookie company had a lot of respect for me after that fiasco. As the saying goes, living well is the best revenge.

Not only was I running the Value Added Services program for the warehouse at this point, I was also quoting on projects, going out on sales calls, invoicing the packaging customers, and even doing collections.

Once a customer got so far behind on paying their invoice that I had to put them on hold, meaning there were no shipments and no production until they paid in full. That was ugly, only to be used as a last resort. The good news was we had their product as collateral—if worse came to worse, we could sell their product to pay the outstanding bill. Thankfully, they paid their invoice and we released their product off hold, but it kind of left a bad taste in everyone's mouth.

Then they decided to pull out all their product without notice. The day before, they requested all the specs and drawings be forwarded to them, so I knew something was up. I had to put their account on hold again till they paid their bill in full, but their drivers were already backed up to our shipping doors. Our dispatcher and the drivers got into a big row, to the point we had to call the police to put a stop to all the madness. An hour later they wired the money into our account, and the product was released.

However, no way was I giving them all the specs and drawings—that was proprietary information, not to be given away to the next packaging company. We got a lot threatening calls, but we stood firm. The next packaging company messed it all up, thinking they could do it for less money, and the result was that they lost a big customer.

CHAPTER 6

The Power of Coupons, Gift Cards and Friends in High Places

One time we had an intricate project—remove outdated coupon books from display boxes and replace them with new updated coupon books. We had to be sure to reclose each display box so that it looked as if no one had taken it apart, repalletize the reworked displays on the same pallets and make sure all the code dates and best-by dates matched.

My job in this was to write up the step-by-step instructions they'd need to accomplish the end result, including updating the system and letting the customer know when we'd completed the project. I clearly stated on the work order that the display box had to be opened from the bottom to remove and replace the expired coupon book, and to tape the display box closed with clear tape.

The problem was the production manager. I was doing my best to get along with him, but he felt he should have gotten my job as he had been with the company for over a year and me only three months. Never mind that he did not have the skill set for the job. He didn't bother to read my instructions, let alone follow them.

He calls me out to the production floor and in front of the whole production crew tells me they can't find the coupons. I looked and found they had all the displays opened from the *top* with all the insides out on the tables. I was so upset at all the time and labor that was wasted on doing it the wrong way.

I grabbed a display box, flipped it over and cut the bottom tape with a knife. I reached in, pulled out the outdated coupon book, replaced it with the new coupon book, taped the display closed and repalletized it. The whole procedure took less than two minutes.

All the women on the production crew started laughing and snickering. The production manager was so embarrassed, he ran to the men's bathroom and slammed the door so hard he broke it off its hinges.

After that he always read my work order instructions and asked me questions if he didn't understand. And to make sure my instructions were being followed, I would be on-site in person for the start of every new project. We both learned a valuable lesson. (Incidentally, all the displays that were opened from the top had to be reworked on our own dime.)

Another time, we received an urgent call from the vice-president of operations at one of the big sports card companies. We had just received ten truckloads of limited edition collector's card vendor boxes, but due to a computer malfunction all the prize cards were stuffed into every fourth box—the other three boxes had no winners in them. This client was paying the reworking invoice and billing it back to the computer company, and we were told to do whatever it took—and whatever it cost!—to get the product re-sorted in one week.

That meant all hands on deck and then some. We had to hire security guards, and had to contact three temporary agencies just to have enough people to work every day. (We knew about a third of the people would not show up so we ordered extras.) We set up 25 production (sorting) lines with over 100 people every day and a security guard for every line. The guards also checked all lunch boxes, clothes and shoes to make sure no one tried to walk out with any of the prize cards. (The prizes included a new sports car and an all-expense-paid vacation to Hawaii for a family of four, so the temptation was there.) We also promised a bonus to every person who stayed to the end and came to work every day.

We not only got the job done, we finished a day early, comfortably in time to ship and make sure the cards arrived before the launch date for the grand opening event. The warehouse management team received a $10,000 bonus.

That was a great example of teamwork. You get results when people care about their work and will make it happen no matter what.

Looking back, though, you can do all the good work possible and it will still amount to nothing if your bosses don't care or don't support you. That was never the case at J&R, and for that I have to thank the J in J&R, Joe Gennaro.

I was very lucky to have Joe as a mentor when I started working in the warehouse business. He and his team took me under their wings and taught me everything about the business, from how to write up a Bill of Lading (BOL), enter a warehouse receipt, track orders or count product for inventories, to how to sit in on—and contribute to—negotiations with potential customers, meeting with them, making dinner plans and talking up the business.

Joe had a gift for getting to know the customers, pinpointing their main concerns and what they expected from us—how to service them and manage their product. Besides getting a good price for storage, potential customers wanted to make sure their product was in good hands and that we could react fast to any quick changes or last-minute emergency orders. Joe was always a good listener and excellent at developing relationships that lasted for decades. To this very day, many customers have remain good friends with Joe.

Following up with customers is always a top priority. Joe knew it, and would send or drop off beautiful packages of wine, chocolates, and flowers. He never forgot a birthday, anniversary or other special occasion and would always send cards. That's one advantage a family-owned and family-run business tends to have—they're more likely to treat people with respect and make them feel like part of the family.

They sure did for me. To this day I have a framed photograph in my home office of the famous Moulin Rouge in Paris, France. with the initials J & R (for Joe and Ruth, Joe's mom and dad). They're standing in front of a shop window with JARDINE written on it. I've kept that photo for decades—I once thought I'd lost it, but then one day I discovered it again in a trailer after David's and my last move. I grabbed it and resolved to never let it out of my sight again.

I have so many great memories of J&R Distribution: all the birthday parties, baby showers, promotions, major holiday celebrations, the pizza parties with the office and warehouse personnel. Lots of fun times. I learned and learned well that you need to take care of your employees, and they will take of you. And I owe that and much more to Joe Gennaro. I'm one lucky girl to have worked under him.

It's so important to take great care of your employees. One of Joe's favorite techniques was to give them gift cards to their favorite restaurants and stores so they could have a dinner out with their family or go shopping for a new outfit. At birthdays and holidays, we all looked forward to receiving those gift cards.

The gift-giving wasn't all one-way either. Once we all decided to make Joe a nice video depicting all of his life accomplishments, his love of the outdoors, fishing and exploring. The video was a hit, and I recommend doing something similar if you have great boss, to show your appreciation. Or if you don't have anyone with video-editing skills, a scrapbook can do the trick.

Someday, when they retire and are sitting in their rocking chair, you will be remembered, and they will know they were loved.

When you work for a warehouse or supply chain company, you learn to take care of each other like they are your second family. The time you spend together can make for a lifetime of memories. You may not always agree with your teammates, but that's okay—if we all thought the same way, we wouldn't need each other.

CHAPTER 7

Union Battles and Other Disappointments

As we grew the non-union packaging business, it really took off, and we needed more warehouse space to add more people and equipment. At the same time, the warehousing union, Local 265, wanted a piece of the action. They passed around a sign-up sheet to all the non-union workers in the packaging side of the business.

Word got out and the owner found out and blew his stack. He had several meetings with the packaging crew to let them know if they tried to unionize the packaging department he would shut it down and move the business far far away. He even rented out a movie theater for all the packaging crew so they could attend without interference from the union warehouse men.

They did not listen and voted for the packaging business to become union.

When I came to work on Friday, the owner was waiting for me and told me not to even sit down in my office. He gave me a stack of checks, told me to go out to the production floor, call them all into the conference room and give everyone their final check. He'd already arranged to close down the production packaging business and move it to Stockton, 57 miles away. It was that far by design—the union only had jurisdiction up to 51 miles so they had no recourse to file a claim to keep the jobs.

It was only a month before Christmas and I felt terrible for them but also felt they did it to themselves. Thank God I had help as all the production crew had to be walked to their cars after they cleaned out their lockers. If looks could kill I would've been dead ten times over. The packaging crew were in disbelief that this was happening. But they had been told—it wasn't my fault they decided to call the owner's bluff.

The whole time, our operations manager was paging me to ask me when it was all clear so he could come pick up all the equipment on flatbed trucks. I was working as fast as I could to get everyone off the property. Finally about 3:30 pm he came in with forklift drivers and our head mechanic to take everything to the new location. We all worked through the weekend to get all the equipment set up and reconnected and we succeeded. It was business as usual on Monday morning. In addition we'd already hired new workers for the production lines and moved approximately 300 pallets to the new location.

A few days later I had my car keyed and my tires slashed. I had a pretty good idea who did it based on the threatening phone calls I'd also received, but there was no way to prove it. Not a fun time.

The nice thing about this was shortly afterward, we picked up a major canned-food company as an account and instantly needed all the space in the much larger warehouse we'd transferred to. In the long run it was a good thing we'd moved.

Of course, acquiring new business is the key to growing any company brand. But with that comes a lot of growing pains, such as hiring additional employees and buying equipment for each of the warehouse locations. This was especially true now that we had two warehouses in the Bay Area and a third in Stockton.

At one point it was a nightmare keeping all three locations stocked with toilet paper and office supplies, not to mention keeping all the birthday party dates straight. It was always company practice to have a birthday cake and a card to sign for every employee for their birthday. Yes, when you work for a warehouse logistics company, you are part of a big family. It's like a cardinal law that you are married to the business and your coworkers, management or not. You all come to work and make it work like NASA sending a rocket to the moon. Maybe not always happily, but for the most part you make sure the containers, truckloads and other projects get completed and delivered on time.

I believe every young person should spend at least two weeks working at a warehouse before graduating from high school. All people know is that they push their shopping cart down the aisle at the local grocery store, put their food in the basket and pay for it at the checkout counter. It's so much more than that, from the manufacturer or grower to the truck, to the warehouse, to another truck, to the distribution centers, then to yet another truck and finally to the stores and shopping malls.

I remember the first time I invited a girlfriend to tour the warehouse. I was working at, she had no idea what I did. All she knew was I worked around food. When I opened the main door to the warehouse she let out a scream so loud that that the forklift drivers came rushing over thinking someone got injured. She had never seen that much food in her entire life and was in shock.

I asked, "Where did you think your food came from?" She'd really had no clue, and it took her a while to get a hold of herself and wrap her mind around it.

But then, I didn't have a clue about some things. Like men. I didn't do a lot of dating after divorcing my husband—as a single mother with a full-time career, I didn't have much time, and after being burned by my ex, I didn't have much inclination. The one time I did, a few years after the union wrangle, tended to prove why I shouldn't.

One of the perks of providing packaging for a big club store is that you get invited to all of the grand openings of new stores. It was at one of these that I met a certain buyer for the chain whom we'll call "Doug." (Not his real name, for reasons that will soon be apparent.)

At this grand opening event there was plenty of food and wine and we hit if off wonderfully. Doug came out to the warehouse to see our packaging operations, and from there we started dating. We had nice dinners and romantic getaways to Napa Valley. I should have picked up on the game he was playing, as we never went out or went away on a weekend—it was always overnight on a weekday and then right back to work. But as I mentioned before, I was naive.

He did send me referrals and I was able to generate new business from them, but I still thought he was hiding something.

It just so happened that they were opening another of their club stores in the area, and I accepted an invitation to the grand opening. Doug asked me if I was attending, but I told him no, that I had a very important customer visiting the warehouse all day that day. (There was no such customer.)

You guessed it, I attended the grand opening. As I was walking into the event I saw Doug standing right next to this very pretty young lady and holding her hand. Well! I walked right up behind him, and when he turned around and saw me he turned white as a ghost—busted!

Then he told me I needed to leave immediately. (The audacity.) I said no, that I wanted to meet the young lady that he was holding hands with. He grabbed my arm and tried to make me leave, but I said to take his hands off of me or I would make a big scene. That's when he came clean and told me that the young lady was his fiancee.

I was heartbroken and fighting back tears, wanting to scream at the top of my lungs and tell everyone that Doug was a dog, but again I stayed professional. I chalked it up to a lesson learned—if it feels good, but your gut tells you that something is not right, pay attention to your gut. Better to bail than to keep going into a big fucking mistake.

About seven months later Doug called me up and told me that his fiancee not only broke off the engagement with him, but that she met someone else and got married within weeks of moving in with him. Furthermore he wanted to know if I would go out with him—any place I wanted to go.

I said no thank you and wished him all the best. It's called karma, baby—he got what he deserved.

CHAPTER 8

Moving on Up

Picking up that big canned-food account out of Sacramento meant that our packaging business exploded overnight. We were running our shrink wrap and bundle equipment 24/7 with no end in sight, and using one of the three warehouses just for packaging projects. This was in addition to three other overflow warehouses we were leasing just to keep up with the growing business. Keeping manpower and paperwork flowing was a nightmare.

It was about this time that we decided to acquire one big warehouse to combine all three warehouses under one roof. We needed at least half a million square feet to start, though, and nothing that size was available. Finally the owner decided to build a new warehouse on the old Spreckels Sugar factory site that was up for sale in Manteca, south of Stockton in California's Central Valley. It was a perfect location, near all the major freeways and close to major distribution centers for a ton of the club store, superstore, supermarket and similar chains. In addition, the land was much cheaper than the Bay Area, with room to grow.

They used dynamite to blow up the Spreckels sign and silos, cleared the land and built a 562,000-square-foot warehouse for what would now be our consolidated business. Back then, in 1990, we were the first warehouse building in that area, the nexus of California State Highways 99 and 120.

Now the whole area is warehouses, including some absolute giants, such as major food producers and Fortune 500 companies. But we were the first.

I got to watch the building process from the very start—laying the forms and bending the rebar to set the foundation, the cranes lifting up the prefab concrete walls. Did you know that when building a place that big (anything bigger than 400,000 square feet) you have to take into consideration the curvature of the earth?! No lie—you need to bend the rebar ever so slightly so as to not have the cement crack or cause structural weakness in the building. Once the building engineer let me look through the surveyor's scope to see the slight bend in the earth's surface—that was incredible. I would drive by the new building every week to check on the progress and it was eye-opening and amazing.

The new building on Spreckels Avenue had its own railroad spur, four rail doors, over 100 shipping and receiving doors, high ceilings, offices up front with a beautiful conference room table that could seat twenty, and an upgraded phone system. It took three and a half weeks to consolidate the other warehouses, working seven days a week and sending out notices to all the customers and carriers that they would all be picking up at and delivering to the new location.

If you can dream it, I've found, the customers will fill it and they did. But let me tell you, it was no easy task.

To top it off, I had my very own office up front by the entrance so I could see all the trucks and visitors arriving. I was finally able to get out of the trailer office in Stockton that I shared with another worker, our desks side by side. One morning, when I arrived at work, he had removed everything off the top of my desk in a mad raging fit, stating he did not have to work with a woman because this was "a man's job" and I had no business being in warehousing and packaging. The operations manager came in wanting to know what all the yelling was about, saw that all my stuff was on the floor off my desk, figured it out quick and told the other guy to pack up and leave until further notice.

That fellow was gone for three days, and came back with a slight attitude adjustment. He treated me much better after that, though there was still a lot of hostility in his voice and body language. Later he would get in trouble again, ranting because I wore dresses and high heels and had lots of pink lipstick and perfume. This time it was with a customer as witness because I was on a conference call.

So needless to say, I was happy to be moving and getting my own office for some peace and quiet. I was not changing myself for him or anyone else—I was not the least bit ashamed of being a woman, and I was not the least bit ashamed of working in warehousing either.

Now that we were all at the new warehouse it was time to install the new racking to utilize all that space, including five-high pallet spots. That's when Mark Hiddleson came in from Specialized Storage Solutions to spec out the footprint of the new building. The actual racking had been sitting in a field that was once part of the old Manteca water slide park—it now had to be transported on flatbed trucks to the new facility. What an amazing undertaking—Mark's installers went to work like precision metalworkers, climbing tall poles and attaching support beams to complete these towers of racking slots. Then all the racks had to be bar-coded with item number information before we could start putting all the product into the slots.

(In addition to being the best in the business at what he does, Mark Hiddleson also hosts a podcast, Tao of Pizza, which you can find on YouTube. I have been on his podcast—look it up.)

The middle of the new warehouse was dedicated to the production packaging equipment so the production manager could have a full view of the production line we were running—the Zambello bundle machine, the high cone, the label line for brite cans, the case packer, the Krones machine for bag-packing the chocolate and hard candy, and everything else. At one time we had over 150 production workers per shift and onsite, with a staffing agency onsite as well to make sure we always had enough people to man the production lines.

After all the racking was installed customers, potential customers were visiting APDS to see what the new operation looked like inside and to meet and greet the staff. They also got to see our new WMS system, upgraded from the old AS/400 system to streamline the shipping and receiving process. By this time we had to handle 120 inbound and 100 outbound shipments per day.

One of my many tasks was updating contracts so they reflected the current warehouse and packaging pricing. I remember traveling back to that big canned-food concern I mentioned earlier every other year to review and negotiate the pack price for each item, and security was paramount. They locked us in the conference room with several of their supply chain team members. If we had to go to the restroom, we were escorted to and from and not allowed to speak to anyone. They bussed us to the company-owned hotel for dinner and to spend the night, and we'd get back up early and do it all over again until we agreed on all the pricing. The grand finale was a celebration at a high-end restaurant with all the executives from the company.

I really enjoyed all the friendships I made with the people there over the years. When they would come to visit in California, we would go wine tasting or go to San Francisco for a night out at a nice seafood or steak restaurant. They'd tell stores sharing how long they had been with the corporation and how they got started in the food business.

When they came out with a new product line they would also come out to California to do line testing on our production line. That was real work and it came down to how many packs per minute, and how fast we could build display pallets for the club stores. Sometimes we'd work late into the night to get our time studies completed.

This went on with other packaging accounts as well and was very time-consuming. But that was just one example of how we made it happen so your food gets from the manufacturer to your table.

CHAPTER 9

Work Is Better with Friends: Adding Transportation to the Mix

We made that place in Manteca a one-stop for all warehousing and packaging services by adding a trucking firm as a partner. The customers were thrilled, and it was a joy to work with the trucking company owner and his team. We already had a history with them. If we needed a last-minute pickup, no problem—the owner would jump into one of his own trucks, pick up the load himself and make sure we had the product before our doors opened at 6:00 a.m. We could get right into production and have it ready for delivery the next day to the big distribution centers. We got so good at it that we would make the appointment with the club store's DC before we even picked up the product. Now that's service with style.

Now our customers could make one call and we would pick up product, FTL or LTL, delivered to us by them, warehouse it, package it, and do all the fulfillment under one roof. That's what made us stand out above the rest of the 3PL providers. We had over 120 customers from all over the U.S. and Europe—most had been our customers for over a decade and always renewed their contacts year after year.

Once we needed to fill one more area in the warehouse with a new customer, so our operations manager said, "go out and do your magic." That meant cold-calling in the surrounding area and bringing back a new customer to fill that spot. I always wore my high heels and a nice dress with a suit jacket, dressed to impress whoever I called on. The problem with cold-calling is you need to get past the gatekeeper, usually the woman at the front desk. So I would always bring little gifts like coffee shop gift cards or a box of gourmet chocolates.

One particular potential customer, a mammoth West Coast food distributor, I'd called on over fifteen times but I could not get my foot in the door to get an appointment. It was always the same lady at the front desk and always the same answer: he's busy and has no appointment times available. So it was time to bring in the big guns: a whopping two-pound box of See's chocolates. You guessed it—she tucked that big box of candy under her desk and told me to take a seat in the lobby. As soon as he was free she would see to it I had five minutes with the big decision-maker himself.

I waited for over an hour and a half, but no luck. She said to come back tomorrow at 9:00 a.m. and she would try again to get me in front of the guy. I got into my car and drove back to my office to call it a day. But when I arrived, the operations manager was standing at the front entrance—he said to turn my car around and get back to the food distributor pronto because the big boss was waiting for me!

Honestly, I don't even remember the drive back from Manteca to the food distributor's base in Tracy, but the head honcho was waiting for me at the bottom of the stairs. He pointed at his watch, said you have five minutes and marched me upstairs to his office. I stood there and gave the most fabulous four-minute speech of my life! He was speechless and said he'd call me in a few days.

Four days later, he called me and asked if we had room for 1,000 pallets of totes and if we could start receiving them in two days?

I asked Aldo if that was doable and he said "hell yes!" We set up the item numbers in the warehouse management system, assign a CSR to the account and lined up full-truckload delivery with the trucking firm. I had also made a friend for life at the front desk, because every year after that I hand-delivered her a big box of top-of-the-line chocolates at Christmastime.

That is how you deliver superior service every time on time. I owe everything to my team and my operations manager—he and the owner always had my back. What a great group—we were a family and took care of each other. I know I got myself into trouble sometimes as I would make promises as a salesperson and overstate some of our services or timelines, but we always made it work.

Of course, sometimes things don't work out as planned. I remember sitting in my office one day and hearing a whole lot of yelling outside by the guard gate. A driver had just picked up a container of chocolates from the Port of Oakland and was trying to deliver it to us. What the driver did not know was the refrigeration unit on the container unit had failed or run out of diesel fuel and the chocolate was running out the back of the container. This container had been in transit for about a month from Switzerland with high-end chocolate, over $350,000 worth.

The yelling? That was because there was a white car stuck behind this container on the freeway and it had splattered chocolate all over this car's front window and hood. The car's driver wanted the delivery driver's information to turn in an insurance claim.

Our security guard wasn't having it. He checked the truck driver's paperwork, told him to go to door 36 and then walk up the steps into shipping and receiving. The guy in the white car was having a fit, for which I couldn't blame him. He called the police and was able to get the truck driver's license plate.

I got the call from our warehouse manager to get out there ASAP and bring my camera. They opened the large swing doors of the container and all this chocolate came pouring out! I sent the pictures to my contact in Switzerland and they approved the rework and cleanup and would pay for it. All in all, we were able to save about half the load, but the rest had to be dumped.

However, a lot of the chocolate couldn't be saved or dumped, because it had run down the manhole. Not only were we not able to recover or dispose of it, but it went into the main sewer line from the warehouse to the street. Two days later we had two gentleman from the city show up at our front door wanting to know why we were putting hazardous material down the sewer line. I was shocked since we had never dumped any hazardous material down our sewer line. Then I remembered the melted chocolate. So we all went out to the manhole and lifted the lid—lo and behold, all that chocolate had hardened overnight, stopping the flow of the sewer. That's what happens when you have hot days and cool nights. It was a hard pill to swallow, as we had to pass the cleanup costs back to the company in Switzerland.

Going forward, we always had the truck drivers open up their doors and check the product inside to make sure there was no damage or any liquid running out the back end. If for whatever reason it didn't look right, we closed the doors, sent the driver on his way and told them to contact their dispatcher. If it looked fixable, we'd send them a price to rework the load and send them an invoice (if they were a customer of ours) or have them pay with a credit card (if they weren't).

Like I said before, the general public has no idea what it takes to get the food from the manufacturers to the stores.

CHAPTER 10

Have You Heard The One ...?

Sometimes the things that can happen around a warehouse are so crazy, I'd think they were made up if I hadn't seen them with my own eyes.

Like the time I was showing one of our candy customers his product in the warehouse and he noticed one of his boxes was crushed on a pallet. It just so happened that this pallet was on the bottom with three other pallets above it in the racks. We all had suspected he wore a hairpiece but were not sure. When he lifted his head up from looking at the crushed box, a nail from the pallet above caught his hairpiece and plucked it right off his head. I laughed so hard I had to walk away and find the operation manager to go over and finish the warehouse tour. We met back in the conference room, finished up the inspection/audit very quickly, and he was on his way.

Or the time we were all sitting in the conference room with one of our biggest customers whose representatives had taken a red eye from New York to California. Their VP of Operations had eaten a tuna melt before boarding the plane. We all could hear his stomach making these weird sounds and he excused himself and was in the bathroom for a very long time. About thirty minutes later he returned to the conference room with the most foul smell we had ever smelled. His boss asked him, "Did you flush and go every time and remove your jacket?" He said no. We had to tell him to go for a walk, remove his jacket and come back when the odor was gone. You could tell he was sick and he really needed to go to his hotel room and skip the meeting, which after another five minutes he finally did. Next day at lunch someone said "Let's order Jack a tuna melt" and everyone busted out laughing. I don't think I've eaten a tuna melt since.

Another time we had produce bins returned from a big club store filled with ten-pound bars of chocolate. While they were unloading the bins off the trailer the forklift driver picked up too much speed and spun around. The whole side of a bin split open, flinging those huge chocolate bars everywhere like edible ninja stars! I managed to jump out of the way, but a coworker wasn't so fortunate—he caught one in the leg and had to go to the hospital to get stitches.

We have a real scare once when we opened up an inbound trailer and there was a white powdery substance on the trailer floor. This was in the spring of 2002, in the midst of the post-9/11 anthrax scare, so everyone went into overdrive. We called the police and they called the FBI and other authorities, and the warehouse was shut down until the men in the white hazmat suits could be called in to assess the powder. Meanwhile, we had to call the carrier and find out where the load originated from and had it been the same driver the whole time.

After several hours we found out the driver had picked up the trailer from his yard where they parked all the trailers after each run. The previous driver was supposed to clean his trailer before he parked it, but didn't. That trailer had been used to pick up palletized fifty-pound sacks of flour.

Sure enough, after testing, the men in the hazmat suits determined there was no threat and we could move forward with loading. Instead we rejected the trailer and told them to provide us with another, clean one, and they did.

The hoops we jump through to make sure the American people receive food that is safe to eat. I could cite a hundred examples, though none quite so dramatic.

In another instance, we had a pickup and the customer chose the carrier. We opened the roll-up door and found chunks of meat on the floor! We later found out this trailer was used to transport meat from slaughterhouses to processing plants for dog food.

Again we refused the trailer, but the driver tried to pull a fast one—he took the trailer to a self-serve power washer and then brought it back to the dock. The stench was so bad we all had to hold our noses—the power washing had only made the smell worse. Our operations manager told the driver to get the trailer off our property and bring back a different trailer the next day. The next day, the driver did come back with a new, clean trailer, and we were able to load him out and send him on his way.

The snag was that our customer blamed us for not loading the trailer from the day before and wanted us to give them a credit on the freight. It was a good thing we took photos of the trailer with chunks of meat on the floor—we had sent an email the day before with the information, and called to let them know what happened the day of the refusal of the trailer, but the messages hadn't gotten through. Since our customer was on the East Coast, the messages were left after they'd closed, and they'd jumped to conclusions rather than check their voicemail or email.

When the dust settled, we all had a good laugh and made a promise to each other to get everyone's after-hours cell phone numbers in case of another emergency. They knew us well enough to know that if we called outside usual business hours it was for a good reason.

Raw meat and mysterious powder aren't the only things we had to worry about, either. We regularly X-rayed cans for a tomato company, checking for foreign material like plastic chips from the augers that crush the tomatoes or broken metal ball bearings from the chopping machines. It's very labor-intensive, as each person had to sit on a chair and watch the X-ray screen intently. If you saw something you couldn't explain, often you had to open the can, pour the contents into a long tray and see for yourself. Sometimes they would let you take a photo of the X-ray screen, send the cans back to the processing plant and they would open the cans themselves and do the inspection.

Once, though, we got an unusual request from the tomato plant to look for some type of pink cloth. We had to spend an entire swing shift, eight whole hours, X-raying about 300,000 cans—and we only had four X-ray machines. We did our best, though, with men and women glued to each screen, swapping them out once an hour so no one got eyestrain. We didn't find it on that shift, and we had no idea why we were supposed to look for such a weirdly specific thing.

We found out the next day, because a rumor like this was too juicy—tomato pun intended—to keep secret. It seems that one of the women on the tomato packing line had a disagreement with her supervisor. She went into the women's restroom, took off her panties, came back out to the can-filling line and stuffed them into a tomato can before they put the lid on it and sent it through the cooker.

Needless to say, the next morning everyone eyes were peeled (yes, another tomato pun) and the hunt was on for the can with the pink panties in it. It wasn't until the end of the week that we finally spotted a can that put a funny image on the X-ray screen. Sure enough, we'd found it. The tomato company people made a special trip to our warehouse, opened the can in front of all of us, and there sat the offending undergarment.

The lady was fired, naturally. And I later heard that from then on, no one on that production line was allowed to go the bathroom without being accompanied by another person.

After things like that happening, nothing surprises me anymore. Once, at a different tomato-processing facility, I saw mice running along the ridge of these big vats of ketchup. One dropped into a vat and ended up getting cooked with the rest of the sauce. That's far less likely to happen today, as there are a lot more regulations for processing food or sauces. But you never know …

Of course, sometimes you have to make your own fun. Warehouses seem to attract their share of merry pranksters, and sometimes it can backfire on them.

Now you need to know when drivers show up late, too early, or not at all we call that a "no-show." If they show up the next day without an appointment, there is a fee, and the carrier needs to pay with a comp check, a credit card, a T-check or cash. Depending on the charge there can be a whole lot of money in shipping and receiving at any given time. The money is turned in to the front office at the end of the day and then goes off to the bank in a drop or lock box.

Also, keep in mind that the operations manager makes the rounds to all the warehouses every day to collect this money, sometimes thousands of dollars. Whoever they assign this job to needs to be trustworthy and reliable.

One day I was just leaving to go to lunch and I looked down and saw this very large envelope on the ground with no markings on it. Hmmm ... what's this? I got into my car and held the envelope up to the light. I was shocked—all I could see was hundreds of dollars in cash with comp checks and T-checks too. So I decided to wait and see if anyone would 'fess up to having lost this envelope.

I left it in my truck and went ahead to lunch, came back about 45 minutes later and went back to work.

Then I saw one of our supervisors walking up and down the hall with sweat beading on his forehead and a look of fear on his face. I'm thinking that this envelope was his and he was looking for it. I'm also thinking "payback time," as he would play jokes on me all the time and I believe in karma. So I put the envelope in my desk drawer and acted like I knew nothing, straight faced and doing my job, working on the computer and making sales calls in my office.

He made several attempts to get my attention and I kept telling him I was very busy and to get out of my office. Our accountant saw the smirk on my face and she figured it out—she asked me to put the supe out of his misery and let him have the envelope. But I said no, make him sweat some more.

Finally, I called him into my office, pulled out my desk drawer and pointed to the envelope, "Was this what you're looking for?" He asked if I'd had this the whole time and said nothing, and I said yes, that's what you get for not being nice to me. Men and their egos, go figure. As it was, he was lucky no one else found the envelope. He knew it, and later he gave me cash for finding it.

I never said another word on the subject, but I always looked around that supervisor's car when I went to lunch or after work, just to be sure no more envelopes were dropped on the ground.

And even when everything is going right, when it's crazy busy and you're averaging over a hundred inbound shipments and a hundred outbound shipments per day, and all is right with the customers and your systems and staff are working in sync, you'll still have one or two employees who shake things up just for shits and giggles.

One time our operations manager ripped into an employee for what was a very minor infraction, and which made him feel so bad in front of everyone. That employee just bided his time … and then one day, he taped a big piece of raw fish under the operation manager's desk. That thing ended up stinking so bad it smelled up the whole front office. Somehow the operations manager knew who did it … but he got the message and never spoke to any of our employees that way again.

And there was the one I was guilty of. Every so often I forgot to bring my lunch to the office—just busy. One day I had back-to-back-to-back customers and no time to even pick up some takeout. But I had been eyeballing this salad in the refrigerator for a couple of days. I asked around as to whose salad it was, but no one knew. Finally I took all the toppings off and made my own salad out of it. It was really good.

Until the next day when I came to work and there was a big sign on the refrigerator door—WHO IS THE THIEF WHO STOLE MY SALAD YOU SHOULD BE ASHAMED AND FIRED! Well, I took the sign off the fridge, then immediately went to the store, picked up the same salad and put it in the refrigerator with an apology note, typed out so the handwriting wouldn't give my identity away.

I never heard any more about it—and I wasn't fired—so I guess it was okay.

CHAPTER 11

Abuse and Fallout

I was feeling very grateful and happy to be moving up the corporate ladder. By then I was living in Blackhawk in a beautiful new condo with my son David and his bulldog Roxey. Life was good, the warehouse was full, and customers were happy.

Then, one evening, there was a knock at the front door.

You have to understand that growing up, I experienced quite a bit of emotional, verbal and even physical abuse. I will not go into who the perpetrators were or what they did, not because I feel the need to hide such things but because I have consulted with some very good attorneys who have unanimously warned me that I would get sued if I told the whole truth. I've had to deal with being sued enough, thanks, as you'll see.

Looking back, what really saved me was 4-H—and not just the hard work cleaning out stalls and riding my horses. I could take off on Saturdays early in the morning after putting food in the crock pot and not return until late at night, often after everyone went to bed. That day just for myself was restorative, kept me busy, and showed me that I could care for others and be cared for.

Suffice it to say that when it comes to children being abused, my antennae are always up. I know the signs, the reactions, and I have zero tolerance for it. I understand no parent is perfect—after all, I am one—but manipulation of a child's mind is a terrible thing to witness, and when discipline goes beyond a motivational slap on the rump to punches to the face, breaking ribs and kicking with cowboy boots, it's not discipline, it's assault.

I opened the door and there was Wesley (not his real name), a friend of David's. He would often come by to play, and I was already on the alert because he often had bruising on his arms and face and black eyes. This night, he was in even worse shape—he looked badly strung out and very smelly. I came to find out that Wesley's father had kicked him out of the house for the third time that year (I hadn't known about the other two times). Wesley's dad was an alcoholic, a drug addict, and had been manipulating and beating him up for many years. Wesley had only found relief in the oblivion of drugs.

Again, no parent is perfect, and here I made a mistake—I told him to go home and try and work it out. That didn't go well. Soon he showed up on my doorstep again in the middle of the night with a broken nose and fresh black eyes. Dear old Dad had beaten him badly and put him back on the streets again.

This time we took him in and fed him, and my son got him cleaned up. He and my son wore the same size clothes, and I had a guest bedroom that he could stay in. Meanwhile I was mentally kicking myself because I hadn't really grasped that this was going on under my nose. I knew Wesley's father, and maybe that was why I hadn't understood the seriousness of what was going on. Well, now was the time to make up for it.

All was fine until Wesley's dad got wind that Wesley was staying with me and all hell broke loose. He would call more than fifty times a day telling me to put his victim out on the streets. He would drive by three or four times a night during the week, throwing empty beer cans with rocks in them at my master bedroom window. I was scared and not getting any sleep, plus going to work every day—it was wearing me and my son down.

Wesley didn't want the police's help, because despite all his father had done, Wesley still loved him and knew he would be picked up and put in jail. Come to find out his dad had a rap sheet four pages long, including the neighbors reporting him beating his son out on the front lawn of his home while intoxicated. But sometimes you need to do the things you don't want to. I contacted Child Protective Services and the local police and filed a report. The police department gave me special protection until I could get in front of the judge and statements from both me and Wesley could be taken.

When I filed the report, that's when things got really dicey. They went to Wesley's dad's home and told him he had to stay 150 feet away from my house and if he didn't he would be arrested. I filed a restraining order too.

Things were quiet for a month. I was told in order to protect myself I need to hire an attorney with a background in child abuse law. So, I did, and it became the best decision I ever made when I got served by the sheriffs for harboring a minor without the permission of said minor's older guardian. I had to get an attorney and appear in Superior Court, which was a whole lot of money to lay out. The attorney had never heard of such a thing: a father suing someone for taking care of his son and keeping him from being beaten multiple times a week.

It didn't help that when we were at a court hearing with Child Protective Services, Wesley's paternal grandmother walks across the room to my side and hands me papers, yelling in this ugly voice that I'd been served. She was suing me for interfering with the "raising" of Wesley, saying that I was not fit to raise my own son, and a lot of other lies and trumped-up charges including molestation. I was sick to my stomach and nearly passed out at the hearing.

No one either of us knew could believe she would do such a thing, all because her drunken relation had her convinced he was correct in trying to beat another relative into submission. This was in addition to the drunk calling my work, telling my boss that I was being sued by him and his mother and trying to get me fired.

It was a good thing I had an understanding boss who knew this guy was lying. He allowed me to attend all court hearings and visits to the child psychologist and therapist. I was never docked any pay—in fact, he gave me a loan to help pay for all the attorney fees, and never rushed me about paying it back (which took me about a year).

Child Protective Services interviewed Wesley's father and grand-mother, then me, my son and Wesley. They later told me in private that the only way Wesley would ever make it to adulthood was if he stayed with me and David, that his dad and grandma were real pieces of work and that in all the years of hearing cases on children they had never come across a case like this one.

The case—eventually—turned out very well. The judge awarded me full custody of Wesley and told his father to stay away from my home, stop harassing me with telephone calls and stop doing drive-bys and throwing empty beer cans at the side of my house at 3 a.m. Wesley lived with me until he was eighteen, then moved in with some friends. He's doing well today. He does still have contact with his father, but like all bullies, his dad is a coward and Wesley is a man full grown, so there are no more attempts at beating him.

I didn't need all of this drama in my life—all I'd wanted was to keep Wesley from being beaten, allow him to live a normal life and to see how nice it was to come home to food on the table and fun without all the yelling and abuse. Looking back, I would do it all over again … except I would have recognized the signs, stepped in earlier, taken more photos and recorded the verbal abuse.

It was a lot to recover from, and took a lot of energy out of me to endure this serious injustice. But now I can come from a place of love and compassion. I feel like I had divine guidance through it—God, a spirit guide, whatever you want to call it—and a wonderful support group, including my boss and my attorney. I learned who my true friends were, and they supported me every step of the way. And I can look back and say that while I wasn't perfect, I did the best I could do with the tools I had.

We are all on this journey of life—in Earth school, so to speak—and have to learn the lessons and move forward, enjoying what life has to offer. Despite all the above events and how they shaped me, I choose to be light and send love to everyone I meet. Even the parents who don't deserve to have children.

CHAPTER 12

Money Owed—No Backing Down

Once we had a big-name company that got three months behind in their payments—over $150,000 in total. I sent emails and voice mails to them for the money they owed us, all of which were totally ignored. Finally I left one more voice mail and forwarded all of the invoices once more, requesting confirmation by the next Friday that they'd received them.

And when I didn't hear back from that company by late afternoon Friday, I put the account on hold. The CSR was informed that no carriers should be allowed to make appointments or pick up any product whatsoever, and if anyone called from the company, to direct the call to me or the operations manager.

You guessed it—they tried to make appointments to pick up their product and were told their account was on hold. I received the call from the company's VP of Operations, who threatened me verbally, saying he was going to physically hurt me and that he would see to it I went to jail and that the company I worked for would be sued for big dollars and so on and so on.

I did not back down and told him to pay up or else, that his product would be kept on hold indefinitely or sold to recoup the past due amount owed to us. He said, "No way, you can't do that!" I said, "Yes, I can—read your contract." He hung up on me.

Within thirty minutes, he and two of his associates—big men all—were in our front lobby screaming and yelling and threatening me and my operations manager. (Nasty potty mouth that VP had.) We put them in the nearest conference room while I made a phone call.

What those jerks didn't know was that I'd called the police the day before and told them there could be a possible serious problem with this company, even giving the PD their names. So when they showed up at our operation, I immediately called the police officer who had been assigned to my case and gave them my name. It didn't hurt that the officer could hear the company reps in the background, yelling and screaming. Three minutes later we had two cop cars on site. Several officers came straight into the conference room, their hands on their gun holsters. The looks of shock on the company reps' faces were priceless!

The police officers told them to leave immediately or go to jail, and I said that I would press charges for trespassing on private property and threatening bodily harm to me and my operation manager. That put a stop to that fiasco. Also, word soon got out in the logistics world: pay your invoices on your product or you will be put on hold.

(Incidentally, a few years later that company went under and declared bankruptcy. Karma at work.)

Going forward, I made it a practice to review all aging reports every Friday. If an account was getting close to sixty days past due, I called them and sent an email warning them that their account could be put on hold. A warehouse operation is not a bank, and certainly not a piggy bank—we don't just give money away. It was in our contracts, which the customers signed, that they needed to pay their invoices within thirty days.

Once we had to put a lien on a customer's product and ended up selling it for ten cents on the dollar, because they didn't pay the storage charges for months on end. Then all of a sudden, they received money from an investor and called us, wanting to pay the past-due storage bill and saying that they had a buyer for their product. Nice try, but we'd already sold it—we only broke even on the move, but it beat losing money.

They predictably threw a hissy fit, but we had it all in writing, and they had been served by the county sheriff, so they had no recourse. They still tried to take us to court, but even their attorney told them not to waste their time. Bottom line: Pay your bills, people, because if you think you can fall behind in your payments and get away with it, your third-party warehouse will sell your product at a discount and move on—all very legally.

A warehouse is like any other business—it needs to make payroll and turn a profit every month, and can't afford to carry non-payers on credit or not have them pay on time. It's also good policy that when a customer pulls out their product, to hold the last two truckloads for any miscellaneous charges that may occur towards the end because once they leave, you will never see your money again. They may even talk bad about you, though that can work both ways. Better to never fall for that trap, and to stay honest at all times.

It's also smart business to make sure you collect all of your money up front, including rework, cross-docking, and anything else that requires your time or warehouse space. If you touch their product, you send them an invoice—your time is money, and you don't work for free. Don't ever do "handshake agreements"—get everything in writing or in an email.

Above all else, keep the money flowing at all times, and remember that it's not fair to the paying customers to make them support the non-paying ones. You are not a charity organization by any means. You can never back down when people owe you money for your services, because you already paid all the labor and took up valuable warehouse space that could have gone to another customer. Don't collect that money, and you'll find yourself unable to take care of anyone else—or yourself.

Think of it as if it were a renter who signs a contract but has no intention of ever paying you, the landlord, and ends up being a squatter. Good luck trying to collect your money then. Just because you have their product already in your warehouse does not mean you will get paid on time—or at all.

You must do your due diligence on every new account. It doesn't matter if they are a big-name company—get on Google, LinkedIn and the credit reporting sites and spend ample time doing a background check. It will save you a lot of sleepless nights. And when they fill out credit check documents—and make sure they do!—get at least three references in writing from past and current customers, and do a background check on them too. (I recommend Dun & Bradstreet for that.) Find out the last place they did business and if they were slow paying or on time.

Sometimes it's a bust no matter what you do. Maybe the customer is poor at marketing or doesn't have a good business plan. You can try to sell their product to the discount stores, but if their brand name is all over the product, you'll have to deal with trademark laws that will prevent you from selling it to anyone.

One habit I got into was first thing in the morning to check on what companies have been sold, acquired, or filed for Chapter 11, 12 or 13 bankruptcy—while hoping none of them was warehousing with my company. If they were, I'd get on the phone with them and get some answers—and usually end up putting their product on hold, not allowing any outbound shipments or customer pickups. If they asked why, I would tell them to call their dispatcher and that I was not at liberty to discuss it.

(If you want more ways to collect your money, contact me. I can't give all my secrets away here, or I'd be out of business.)

Keep all this in mind the next time you push that shopping cart around your favorite store. Know that a whole lot of warehouse and operations people spent countless hours, including overtime, to get your groceries to market. That's time away from their families and weekends given up just to meet the deadlines or the shelves go empty. Not to mention charge-backs from the major grocery chains if they don't deliver on time, or if the shelves are empty for just one day—there goes all your profit.

I ask you, do you really appreciate the grocery stores and other big-box and club businesses? I do, and I have a great appreciation for all warehouses and 3PL operations across the United States and elsewhere.

CHAPTER 13

Scandal and Bankruptcy

If you have ever experienced bankruptcy, you know how it affects you psychologically, mentally and physically. Now imagine instead of a personal bankruptcy, a corporate one that involves big food manufacturers and national and international accounts.

This took place in the early 2010s, when the third generation of the family that owned the warehouse business decided at the last minute they did not want to carry on the family tradition. Keep in mind this kid had been put through the top colleges, had all their expensive vacations paid for, received a huge down payment on an estate home so his new bride could live the good life that most people could only dream about, and got to buy all the toys he could want—nice cars, jet skis, and trailers and trucks to tow the play things around—all in the expectation that he would one day run the family business.

It broke the owner's heart, and all the workers and executives did their best to rally around and support him until he could find someone else to run the company. We were really hoping he would pick the current vice president of operations and give him a percentage of the business as a sign-on bonus, as he was good at his job and everyone really liked him. That way the owner could ease his way out of the company but still have control and be one of the shareholders that oversaw important decisions.

Things were very quiet for about two months. We all figured the owner was working out the details of the transition, as he was interviewing several candidates and apparently getting ready to make a final decision.

Then came the shock of a lifetime, one that turned my life upside down. I received a call from one of our top customers, who put me on speakerphone and wanted to know why I had not shared with them that we had filed for bankruptcy. When they demanded, did I plan on telling them?

What the Hell were they talking about?! I didn't know of any bankruptcy and I was convinced they had made a huge mistake. It was like someone had kicked me in the stomach—I couldn't even breathe! They would not stop asking me questions I couldn't answer. They said they were flying out the next day with their corporate attorney, and that I'd better have a plan of action in place, including a new location where we planned on warehousing their product.

Just then our VP of operations came out of his office and gave me a Look. He asked me what was going on and did I know of any bankruptcy? I said no and that I too had just received a customer call wondering why I hadn't told them about us filing for bankruptcy.

The VP and I called the owner and left a message on his voicemail to call us back, saying that it was an emergency. (An understatement!) Then we called the company CPA, got no answer and left another message. It was like all the higher-ups were on vacation. Meanwhile, more calls were coming in from our customers, wanting to know what was going on and was their product safe, were we going to still be shipping orders out or were they going to come and find our front doors chained up. For two whole days my phone rang off the hook with customers asking about the bankruptcy, what was the plan, when was it going to be announced and on and on. And there was literally nothing I could tell them, because nothing had been told to me.

Finally on the third day, we heard back from the owner and the CPA. Yes, in fact the owner did file for bankruptcy, in an attempt to reorganize. But I wasn't buying it—my gut told me something else was going on. Our profit-and-loss (P&L) reports were good—we were making money every month, especially in production. But while we had funds in our bank account, the amount was unusually low, and we were barely making payroll every week. Where was all the money going?

I came to find out that the owner of the company had a big falling-out with the owner of the building because repairs to the building had been delayed or not performed as requested. In retaliation, the company owner hadn't been paying the rent, and was now six months behind in the payments. You never, *never*, NEVER stop making payments on a multi-million-dollar building just because of a disagreement! This building had been built to the company owner's specifications, including a perfectly executed racking system, temperature control, a state-of-the-art IT system, a shipping and receiving office in the middle of the building, two roll-up doors to receive flatbed trucks, over 100 doors in all, a driver lounge and plenty of trailer parking. (Not to mention a well-seasoned team where everyone would step up to tackle any major issues—the same team whose payroll we were barely making.)

My blood pressure was going off the charts because of all this—my doctor had to put me on a higher dosage of blood pressure medication. For the most part, I wasn't sleeping well (sometimes on the weekends I could catch up a few extra hours). But I was coming up with a plan, one that I did not share with anyone. For starters, I had secured several other 3PL warehouses that would help me out should the current warehouse get padlocked. Once I had those options set up for the current customers, I could focus on who out of the potential buyers would actually purchase our company at Superior Bankruptcy Court two months hence.

Within one month, it had narrowed down to two 3PLs (a third had dropped out of the running).

Things were starting to heat up with one of them especially, a national logistics company who wanted a bigger footprint in Northern California and to add it to their website as well. At this point I'm still receiving a paycheck from my owner—on time and with no hiccups thanks to the dictates of the bankruptcy court—and keeping very close to all of our accounts so there are no more surprises.

Then I received a call from that national 3PL company, wanting to meet with me offsite to offer me a job, go over my salary and find out what it would take for me to make the switch. I met with the VP of Operations and the President of Sales, it was a great meeting and we came to an agreement on all points—my salary, plus a percentage of every sale and every new customer I signed up to come over to the new company. I told them to draw up the contract and that I'd review it with my attorney and get back to them with any questions.

The very next day, the President of Sales called and asked me how many of our customers had I signed up with their contracts, on their letterhead with the exact same warehouse rates? I said, rather harshly, what the fuck?! I had just finished redoing all the contracts that night and early that morning. Now I needed to call every account, explain to them what was going on, send them the new contract on a PDF, and give them my word that I was going with this other 3PL, that they would be well taken care of with no interruption of service and I would be there to support them all the way?

Again, something wasn't right. I still hadn't received my contract from this company, and when I kept asking them about it they would tell me their attorney was reviewing it—as soon as he approved it they would send it over to me to sign and date, effective immediately.

Within a week I had all eighty-two accounts set up with the new 3PL contracts. But what I did not share with them was that I told every one of those accounts not to sign anything until I myself had signed on with this new company. I still did not trust them—it seemed like they were stalling, buying more time. This dragged on for another two weeks and still no contract for me.

Then I found out from one of my customers that the President of Sales was calling all of my customers behind my back and had signed up two of my major accounts! He also told them I was already on board and that I would be their main contact. Now I got the picture—it had all been lies just to poach our customers under false pretenses. I still had no contract with them, and it seemed clear that I never would—any talk of a contract had just been BS.

A week before the court date, the national 3PL had a big meeting scheduled at 7:00 a.m. at a local restaurant. I was there, my heart beating out of my chest. It was all I could do to hold it together, because a) now I knew their game, and b) I had a secret weapon. The night before the meeting, a very dear friend of mine called me—his girlfriend worked for an attorney that specialized in corporate bankruptcies and acquisitions. He told me that this company who'd offered to sign me would not be buying us after all—they'd changed their minds, stating it was too much money at the time for them. This confirmed what I knew: that they were just using me to get all the accounts signed up with them and moved into their warehouses.

What they also didn't know at this 7:00 a.m. meeting was that I had a 2:00 p.m. meeting that same day with the other 3PL company looking to buy us. They were flying out that morning in their private jet, with a cashier's check for the total purchase amount for the company that I'd worked for over twenty years. And they *would* be at Superior Court the next week, to become the new owner. Meanwhile I still had my other eighty accounts on the fence, waiting for me to tell them where to go or to just stay put in the current warehouse until the new owner took over. I turned off my phone for the rest of the day because I knew

I was going to be in a meeting with the new owners, and negotiating my salary and terms of our agreement with them.

When I arrived at home that night, I turned on my phone and there were—yes, I counted them—*thirty-seven* voicemails from the President of Sales of the national 3PL company, most of them telling me to check my emails for their contract with me and that I'd better sign it and send it back ASAP! Just before I went to bed, I received call #38 from this jerk, And he wasn't subtle—"You'd better sign the contract and send it back or we are going to sue you, and we will make sure you lose your home and everything else and you'll never work in warehousing business again," and on and on in that vein.

Just to be on the safe side, I opened up and read the contract, and the BS I'd gotten from him before was nothing compared to this! It wasn't even half of what we had agreed on, and my commission was not even close to what he'd promised—something like 0.5%.

Shortly thereafter he called me again, and I wasn't subtle either—I told him to go fuck himself.

Thankfully I knew I would be working for the other 3PL company, who would now be the only bidder in bankruptcy court. I didn't get much sleep that night, maybe two hours, but the next morning I called all eighty of my remaining customers and told them whatever they did, don't sign any contracts with the national 3PL company. They weren't going to get any more of my accounts.

It pretty much worked out. I signed on with company #2, kept all my accounts, and even got my old office back … minus all my files. Or at least that's what I let my former employers think.

I had started to box up all my customer files when I heard we were going through bankruptcy, knowing they would be a valuable asset to whoever bought out the company. Also, there was a lot of personal information on our customers in there: private cabin numbers, ex-wives' contact information, emergency contacts, mistresses' names … you see where I'm going. This was information I'd given my word I would never share.

I began taking the boxes home, a few at a time, until everything started going south and I need to remove the rest of them from my office in a day. I managed to get a coworker's help to load them into my car, and thankfully he never asked what was in the boxes—he would've been blown away if he'd known he was handling over 25 years of customer contacts and private information.

Especially since the next day, the same guy walked into my office and told me to clean out my desk and go join the unemployment line. Which I did—a half-hour later I told him I was done and would be leaving.

Before I could go, he started opening up all the now-empty file cabinets and yelling at me, asking where all the blankety-blank files were. I couldn't resist—maybe I should've, but I couldn't. "Don't you remember? You helped me load them all into the back of my company car yesterday." He flipping lost it and demanded I bring them back. I said it was too late, and they were all in a safe place. (Really, what was he going to do, fire me?)

Worse still for him, I'd already returned the company car to the warehouse with the keys in it. A good friend had given me a ride there and was still waiting for me in the parking lot to take me home, because while I had my own car, I didn't want my now-former bosses to know about it. (Just being cautious.) I drove my own car that night to meet with the new owners and they hired me on the spot. The next day I was back in my old office and it was business as usual, except for spending the next four days typing up new warehouse agreements with the new owners' name on all the contracts.

And where had I hidden all those files? Well, the new owners never asked, and I never told—in fact, I'm still keeping that to myself. A girl's gotta have some secrets ...

CHAPTER 14

Safety First

One afternoon I had just left my office and was walking out the door to get in my truck when I heard my name being called—or, rather, screamed in panic. Our controller had just slumped over in her chair and was not breathing, her eyes rolled back in her head. Her body was sliding down the side of the chair, and when I arrived I could see her head was going to hit the floor first and hard. I grabbed one of her arms and pulled her up to break her fall.

I yelled at two people to call 911 immediately, but after about 45 seconds no one came back to me to confirm that they had. I began CPR—breathing assistance and chest compression—as there were no signs of a heartbeat or respiration. (Remember, my father had been a fire marshal when I was growing up, so I was certified and trained to do CPR, thank God.) I knew this was very serious and I was losing the battle to save this woman's life.

Thankfully, one of my coworkers (not one of the ones I'd told to call 911) came in with her phone in her hand. She had the emergency dispatcher on the line and held it up to my face so I could give them the rundown of what was going on. I told them we needed the paramedics and the fire department ASAP! My arms were getting tired and I was running short of breath, and to top it off, I was dealing with the controller's garlic breath due to the Chinese food she'd had for lunch.

Magic to my ears were the sirens on the fire trucks and the ambulance right behind them, about two minutes later. (The fire department was only a block from our facility.) Those two minutes had seemed like twenty to me because CPR is hard work. Regardless, the angels were looking over us that day.

By then, the poor controller had released all of the usual bodily fluids, front and back. We kept telling everyone to stand back and give the paramedics room to work on her. They put an oxygen mask on her face and lifted her body onto the stretcher, then into the ambulance. Mercifully, by then they had gotten a faint heartbeat and air was being forced into her lungs. She was back from the brink of death

I followed the ambulance to the nearest hospital's emergency room. After the doctor examined her, it was determined she'd had an aneurysm—it ran in her family's history. The hospital wasn't equipped to handle this kind of emergency, and she needed an operation right away, so she was airlifted to Stanford Medical Center, where they had a special unit just for aneurysms.

On my way back from the hospital, I had a revelation: what the Hell would have happened if I'd had a heart attack or needed CPR? No one else at work had been trained to do CPR or even had basic first-aid training. I knew from my training that the first few minutes are so critical to help save a life.

By the time I got back to work I was fuming. My operations manager walked into my office, told me what a great job I'd done … and then saw the look on my face and asked me what was wrong. My response: "Who the hell is going to save my ass?!" He realized what I meant and said, "You're right, Judy, I'm so sorry—I never thought about it that way."

I also pointed out that the two guys I'd told to call 911 had taken off and never came back to tell me that they'd done so, that the fire department or paramedics were on their way, nothing. So the operation manager calls the two fellows into his office with me there, and they started crying. They'd both panicked, ran into the warehouse and started telling everyone about what was going down in the front office, but totally forgot to call 911. Go figure—some people do strange things under pressure.

The next day we had a plant-wide meeting, including everyone in the office, all the upper management and everyone in production, to go over what had happened the day before. They set up CPR training with the local fire department for the following week, with people from each department so we would have coverage in all areas of the warehouse.

It took a real emergency to finally bring it to people's attention that we needed CPR training. But we all started feeling a lot better going forward with our everyday duties. All businesses, including warehouses, should make it mandatory to have CPR-trained personnel onsite and have ongoing training for those personnel.

Nor were life-and-death concerns confined to the warehouse. In the early 2000s I spent a lot of time traveling to meet with customers and going to fancy food and candy trade shows. It was a lot of fun. Plus you can meet with your current customers, take them out to dinner and let them know how much you appreciate their business, and visit their corporate offices to talk to their CEO and teams.

Not to mention all the samples and free gifts that I received at these shows, which I would bring back to my team—full-sized candy bars, gift bags, totes, T-shirts, gift cards and 25% discount coupons. I always made sure to share these goodies with all my team members.

It wasn't all sweetness and light, though. On one of my return trips from a candy show in Chicago, I missed my connecting flight and arrived in Sacramento at 3:00 a.m.—not a good time to retrieve your car from long-term parking. The airport shuttle driver dropped me off, watched me walk to my car, open the door and get in.

What I didn't know was that when I left my car there seven days before, I'd left my lights on. My battery was dead—not a little bit low, but completely drained. All I got when I turned the key was a faint clicking noise. Crap.

Suddenly, I saw this guy at the side of my car! He came to the window and said "Hey, lady, I can help you—open your door and I can help you." I was not about to open my car door. Aside from him being a complete stranger, the smell of him was awful, even through the closed door. He stank like an open grave—dirt and rot. Oh, Hell, no!

Once he figured out I was not opening my door, he got very upset and started pounding on the window and hood. At this point I'm scared out of my wits and praying he didn't have a weapon or an ax to break into my car and kill me. He went on like that for over fifteen minutes, which felt like an eternity. Meanwhile, I discovered there was no cell phone service in the parking lot, because the Sacramento airport is out in the boondocks! I kept trying to call 911 with no response, and thinking someone was going to find me raped and beaten to death or with a knife through my heart.

Just then the airport shuttle came by again, and I prayed to God that the driver would look my way. Finally I caught a break—the driver stopped and stayed there, watching me. I started yelling at the creep beating on my vehicle, thinking I'd better make some noise or I was going to die. Then the shuttle driver shone a light at my car, and the creep ran off.

Three minutes later, the airport police were there and gave my car a jump to get it running again. They told me they'd had a lot of break-ins at that lot, and had been hearing about some skeevy guy following people back to their cars in the early morning when they got dropped off by the shuttle. It was nice to know they were on the case—though I wished they'd arrested the creep already.

It was a wake-up call for me and I made some major changes in my life. I spent the next two and a half years taking karate classes, eventually reaching black-belt status. I loaded my car with two flashlights, extra batteries, a compact instant jump-starter, a fire extinguisher (to blast the bastards, and also in case of fire), a handheld rocket launcher like the ones they keep on boats in the ocean that I could fire into the air via the sunroof, and a gadget where you pull a pin and it lets out an ear-piercing screech.

Just for safety's sake, I added can of hair spray. (You might laugh, but my brother John showed me a lit match can turn a can of hair spray into a miniature flame thrower. I tested it and it worked! Just make sure the nozzle is pointed away from you.)

God saved me that morning, but I wasn't going to take any more chances. To all the women who travel a little or a lot, take my advice: take precautions to protect yourself, and be aware of your surroundings at all times. Especially late at night in the middle of nowhere.

CHAPTER 15

He Died Doing What He Loved

I was grateful to have worked with and been mentored by one of the best operations managers who ever lived. "Steve" (not his real name) taught me about patience, how to deal with frustration, and that everyone has their own battle going on at home or in their life.

I met Steve back in 1992 when he was in charge of procurement and acquiring bids for projects. He was a family man, married with a very young daughter who was as cute as a button. He loved BMWs, was always honest and had a gift for fixing just about any kind of equipment. And if he couldn't fix it, he knew who to call that could.

He was slow to trust anyone, as you had to earn his trust. But once you were his friend, he had your back. He always worked out the details when acquiring new or used warehouses, getting fair terms and pricing, reading the fine print and rereading it.

Once I picked up a new customer overnight who had 25 truckloads that needed a home the next day. Steve got to the warehouse by that afternoon, but the owner of the warehouse was out of state and had the only keys to the building. Steve contacted the landlord for permission (and the keys), then brought bolt cutters, called a locksmith, and we were in that building in less than an hour. By late afternoon we had all 25 loads unloaded and entered into the WMS system, all the necessary information forwarded to the customer, and all paperwork taken to our corporate warehouse by myself or shuttle drivers.

Customers loved Steve. He had a way about him that, no matter what the situation, he could come up with a solution that worked for everyone. He treated everyone with respect at all times. And being in California, it certainly didn't hurt that he spoke fluent Spanish.

He made sure we had birthday parties for everyone who worked in the warehouse, including the production team. And the company picnics were the best! In addition to a full menu—hamburgers, barbecued chicken, ribs, and hot dogs for the little kids—there were prizes for everyone. No one walked away empty handed. And not cheapo prizes either—TVs, boom boxes and gift cards, just to mention a few, made sure that people were happy with the gifts. The only problem was that people started to bring their extended family, and the company picnic was meant for the employees only, so we had to set some guidelines.

Steve was all about giving people a second chance, but they had to earn his trust. One example: we had a warehouseman get caught stealing food out of the damaged area, which was where we kept product too banged up to be shipped. We held it there until the customer had it dumped or wrote a ticket to release it, whereupon we would offer the goods to our employees or Second Harvest Food Bank. It turned out this guy was taking stuff because they were poor and he was desperate to feed his family—he had a wife and two kids.

What Steve did next was amazing. First he wrote up the employee, put the write-up in his file and gave him a 90-day probation. But then he put a care package together for that employee's family, plenty of food plus gift cards to local grocery stores. He wanted to teach the employee to talk to him, the operations manager, about any issues, and that he would not be judged, especially when it came to family issues.

The employee was very grateful. And after 90 days Steve removed the write-up from the employee's file and never spoke of it again.

Steve definitely had a sense of humor. Sometimes he would get me laughing so hard that I had to walk into another room to get myself under control.

He was also no stranger to getting backlash or being questioned by certain members of our team, because sometimes he did things outside of the normal. Once he ordered an entire truckload of shrink wrap film for wrapping pallets, far more than we'd normally stock, and he took some heat for that. But there was a method to his supposed madness—he had heard the price of gas was going up soon. Shrink wrap is plastic, and most plastic (like gasoline), is made of petroleum. So when the price of petroleum, crude oil, goes up, the price of gas goes up AND the price of shrink wrap goes up substantially.

When Steve placed the shrink wrap order, it was at the old price, but three weeks later it had jumped over 20%. By placing that big order when he did, he saved a ton of money for the company. In addition, we increased our pallet wrap price to our customers, matching that of our competitors—but since we'd bought our wrap at the lower price, we were making more profit than them.

Then we got another benefit, because with the price increase in crude oil, it cost more to make plastic, so less shrink wrap was being manufactured. There was an industry-wide shortage of the stuff ... but thanks to buying so much already, we never ran out of shrink film for our customers. The price didn't come down for about three months, and by then we'd stolen a march on our competitors. That truckload kept us going for several months through the oil crunch.

All tours and visits by customers had to be run by Steve first, along with the dates and times they would be visiting so we could provide safety vests and have them sign an NDA. Photo IDs were required for every visitor, along with a business card or second form of ID, before they were allowed in the warehouse or production floor. And no photos were allowed whatsoever.

You need to understand that operations managers of 3PL warehouses have a great responsibility for the good of the owners and the whole team. Most are on call 24 hours a day and respond to all kinds of things, like false alarms, injured workers, disgruntled employees, loss of power or internet ... the list goes on and on. And Steve handled it all.

Once Steve told me, "If you thought like me, I would have never hired you in the first place. I want someone to think outside of the box and report back to me. I want a woman's point of view. I also want you to see the end results of your actions and play it out in your mind before you make your final decision. Then run it by me and we will figure out the best plan of action."

Steve had been working for the company for about five years and there were a lot of changes going on due to new ownership. We noticed he was not happy about some of them—many of the requests the new owners were making on him were unreasonable. He was under a lot of stress and looking more and more tired. He was also spending more time on the phone with the bigwigs back east than running the day-to-day operations.

One afternoon he came into my office, half-closed my door and told me he didn't know how much longer he could work under all that pressure. He admitted he was so stressed it was affecting his sleep and his relationship at home. The company was demanding more profits with less people, and the people we were training in the warehouse would stay just long enough to learn the ropes, then leave for a higher-paying job once they were certified to drive a forklift or fill other positions.

And no wonder. The owners didn't give any wage increases for over two years, with the cost of living going through the roof. Our best people, our veterans, went first, leaving for positions with more paid medical benefits and lower co-pays. I would hear from people who left that they found other jobs very quickly. They would tell me they should've left sooner because their new employer treated them with respect and they felt like family.

We started working with more staffing agencies at the company's behest to cut costs. Sometimes the people the agencies sent wouldn't even show up, leaving us short-handed and unable to complete projects on time. This created more problems, like starting late on the next projects in line, creating a domino effect. In order to catch up we would often have to work Saturday overtime on our dime.

It broke Steve's heart as he did everything he could to try to fix things, despite the CEO and board working against him. I talked to him several times about his health and that he needed to see his doctor, that no job was worth all this stress. He did start looking for another job, but perhaps not soon enough. One evening on his way out the front door, I stopped him, said he looked terrible and pleaded with him to go get medical help.

That night he had a massive heart attack and was rushed to the emergency room. They put him on life support, but five days latter it was determined that he was brain-dead and took him off. That company killed him as surely as if they'd put a gun to his head. And I promised myself no company would ever put that kind of stress on me, ever! Steve had loved his work, but look what had happened to him.

Having the right boss early in your career is a blessing, and helps you to get a solid footing and build confidence early on. I'm glad Steve was there for me.

CHAPTER 16

Who Can You Trust?

In 2008 I was made an offer I couldn't possibly refuse. A big East Coast investor was opening a logistics firm in Stockton, just up the road from Manteca, and wanted to make me Vice President of Sales, complete with stock options and the like. This sounded like a great deal—a chance to move up from being "just a salesperson" to the executive suite, to smash the glass ceiling.

It was a great deal—for the first two months. Then everything went downhill, fast.

The first weeks of starting a new company have all the joy of starting a new relationship—the adventure, the novelty of discovery. We hired a veteran operations manager who really knew his stuff, brought in some temps to do shipping and receiving, accounting, warehousing. We were on the ground floor of the operation and dreaming of big things. When we got our first customer, a local vegetable canning company, we were so excited.

And then ... nothing. I was working my sales magic like mad, talking to one potential customer after another. They would be really interested in working with us, and I would go back to the office and prepare for the new clients coming in. Then those same companies would call me back and say they were sticking with their current 3PL firm, or they'd decided to go in another direction. It was starting to get baffling—here we were with great backing and a lovely warehouse and we couldn't get anyone in save for that one canning company.

Finally one potential customer unbaffled me, telling me they'd decided to go elsewhere because they'd done a background check on our CEO—the "big East Coast investor"—and didn't like what they saw. The person I was talking to was a longtime friend in the industry, and told me I should do some research on who I was working for. (In retrospect, I should've done so before taking the damn VP job in the first place, but I'd been so dazzled by those two letters. Live and learn.)

Well, I did my own checking, and I didn't like what I saw either. The man had a long record of being a con artist, running Ponzi schemes and the like. He had been doing this on the East Coast, but had burned so many people there that now he was having to uproot to the West Coast to keep it going. He was driving around on a suspended license—actually, on FOUR suspended licenses from different states, none of them California. His wife, who was supposed to be involved in the business and filing much of the paperwork, wasn't doing so, even though she kept saying she had or promising she would.

And now the man was trying to blackmail our one and only customer, saying they needed to pay just a few days after receiving our invoices (the agreement was that they had 30 days). Being unable to lure in other suckers, our CEO was getting desperate for cash—we'd already had to let the shipping and receiving guy go, then the accountant, because we couldn't pay the temp agencies.

And then came the hammer blow. I got a call from the CEO's landlord—he was renting a home in California. The landlord told me our head honcho was laid out on the next doors neighbor's lawn and not moving—they thought he might be dead. They asked that I come check on him, and if I didn't they were calling the cops.

Needless to say, I went to investigate and found him just as the landlord had described. He was so drunk he didn't even recognize me. I had to drag him into the house and get him to bed to sleep it off. Come to find out that in addition to all his other "qualities," the man was a full-blown, around-the-clock alcoholic. At work, he always had a water bottle, but he was filling those bottles with vodka and Sprite. And from Friday night to late Sunday afternoon, he would get so smashed he couldn't function, and would do things like ... well, like pass out drunk on the neighbor's grass.

Enough was enough—I had to pull the ripcord and fast. I contacted our one customer, apologized and let them know I'd made a very bad decision to go into business with this piece of shit. Thankfully I knew where the CEO had hidden the spare set of keys to the warehouse, so the next Friday night I got them and opened the building, including all the dock doors and the front entrance gate. By 3 a.m. Saturday all the customer's product was ready to move. Their drivers worked from before dawn until late Saturday evening and pulled every pallet out of the warehouse.

Monday morning, the CEO finally showed up and flipped out when he saw all the product gone. I told him what had happened and what I'd done. Of course he told me I was fired, but I replied that he couldn't fire me—I'd already quit! I had even turned in my company car, filled with gas and cleaned spotless. I'd only showed up that morning because I wanted to see the scumbag's face and give him his keys back.

What a piece of work. To this day, I am stunned that I'd ever believed him. I guess I'd been so dazzled by the promise of a vice presidency, I couldn't see what I was being made VP of. By the end, six months later, I was just happy to be out from under that liar, with my reputation in the industry intact.

(I did get one benefit from the whole mess—meeting up with Ray Anselmo, the erstwhile shipping and receiving guy. He wasn't that experienced in logistics, but man, could he write a business letter or organize a spreadsheet. He's been doing freelance work for me ever since—including rewriting and editing this book. He told me more than once that I should write a book about my experiences as a woman in the logistics business ... and now here it is!)

Of course, when you have enough experience in any industry (and don't burn your bridges) you'll be in demand regardless of the circumstances. Other companies had been recruiting me the entire six months I'd been VP of Sales for the failed startup, and when I realized the full measure of the disaster it was, I took one of them up on their offer. I literally gave the scumbag his keys that Monday morning and went to my new job—didn't miss a day's work.

I spent about a year and a half at the next company and really enjoyed working there—except for one person. Madge (not her real name) hated my guts, for reasons that to this day are a mystery to me. And she didn't restrain herself to dirty looks and snide comments. Once she sabotaged one of my accounts by paying the order puller to pull the wrong item and code date just to get me in trouble. The product was yeast for fermenting wine. It has to be added to the wine at just the right time, when the sugar content hits a specific point—there's a very small window for the vintner to do that.

I received a 6 a.m. call from the winery in Napa, over two hours away from the warehouse, telling me I sent them yeast for Chardonnay when it was supposed to be for Cabernet Sauvignon—different vintages use different yeasts. They needed to add the right yeast RIGHT NOW, or in a few hours the whole batch of wine would go to shit.

I jumped in my SUV, wearing my Victoria's Secret PJs with a coat thrown over them. I called ahead to the warehouse, telling the operations manager I was coming in hot to pick up the right yeast, giving him the lot, the date code and everything else, and to have it ready because I needed to deliver it to the winery in Napa as fast as I could drive it there. When I told him the name of the winery, he said they'd delivered that yeast with that lot and date code the previous day. I said to just pull it and I'd explain later—since I didn't have an explanation yet. Thankfully, he had it ready and on the dock when I arrived.

Somehow—I don't remember how—I made the two-hour-plus drive to Napa in an hour and ten minutes! My contact there was amazed I didn't get pulled over by the California Highway Patrol. Everyone else there was standing outside, looking at me in shock. But that's what I had to do, or our customer would've had a huge claim for our spoiling four entire vats of Cabernet.

I told my contact to show me what we'd delivered the previous day, and sure enough, it was yeast for Chardonnay—someone on our end had screwed up. My head spinning, I called our operations manager, told him what had been delivered and sent him photos of the product on the pallet. He did a cycle count and found we had way too much inventory for Cabernet. That's when the order puller confessed that Madge had bribed him to send the wrong product in order to get me in trouble.

Seriously, who does that?!

Needless to say, I was raging when I pulled up to the office after my return from Napa (at a more reasonable speed). Madge saw me coming, took off running and locked herself in her office. Amazingly, she wasn't fired for almost ruining a customer's product—the operation manager just suspended her for three days without pay.

But things were never the same there for me. I made it a rule from then on to always check my orders on the dock that were staged to be picked up that night or early the next morning—I wasn't giving Madge a second chance to pull that stunt. I never had a problem with the owner or any of the other higher-ups—it was that one bitch that caused all the problems. Finally I figured out that they weren't going to give her the sack, and that the trouble would continue until one of us left. And Joe Gennaro wanted me back. So I quit and went back to APDS.

But karma has this way of paying things forward. Ten years later I received a call from the owner of that company, begging for my help. Madge was suing him for back wages—and over a million dollars in commissions on accounts *I* had brought to the company! Of all the nerve!

See, I had secured five very large accounts during the year-plus I was there, and had left them all behind when I left to get away from Madge, like an animal gnawing off its own leg to escape a trap. Within six months I started receiving calls from three of those accounts, saying they weren't happy and wanted to transfer their product to APDS. I said I needed to honor my word to the previous company, so they had to prove to me they weren't being treated fairly. Boy, they sure weren't! I could not believe my ears at the stories I was told—that company had turned into the Wild West, every person for themselves. And it was largely due to Madge.

Those three accounts did end up moving their product over to APDS, and I made sure to give them the attention they deserved. But for Madge to try and claim commissions for those accounts that not only I had brought to that company, not her, but that she did everything possible to drive off within months of my departure … oh, that was rich.

And now the owner needed me to take a deposition with his attorney, who would be calling me in a few days. I'd like to say I resisted the temptation to say "I told you so." But I didn't—I told him point-blank that I'd warned him not to trust that bitch and that one day she would be suing him. Not gonna lie, it felt good to be vindicated.

I did take the deposition with his attorney, and about three months later I took the witness stand on the owner's behalf during the suit. When Madge's eyes met mine in the courtroom, she knew all her lies would be exposed. And they were—the judge and the jury saw right through her bullshit. The company won the case, and Madge got nothing. I almost felt sorry for her. Almost.

Bottom line: if you're not happy with your employer, it's better to just leave and find a job where you are happy. Know your values and your skill set, and keep building them—through continued education, special training, attending seminars, listening to TED talks, whatever. (I do love TED talks.) Never stop learning.

Those are the steps I took, and I didn't spend a day out of work for decades. And every time I moved on I made more money. I knew I could bring in sales no matter where I went, and I did.

CHAPTER 17

The "C" Word

Over the next year the warehouse hired three operations managers, all of whom failed. Finally they promoted someone within the company and he managed to get things back on track—almost. The man had no people skills and yelled all the time. I was constantly getting phone calls from our customers telling me he was hard to talk to, that it was his way or no way. I actually felt sorry for him—he was doing his best and he was smart, but he had no business talking to customers. Even the people in the office had a hard time talking to him.

Once we went out to lunch with a customer and our CSRs and they all said the new operations manager was yelling all the time. I wanted to crawl under the table and try and forget it ever happened. When the customer got back on the road to return to his office, he called me on his cell and told me I had better do something about his behavior or he would.

Every week I was receiving calls and texts from customers stating he was not returning calls in a timely manner, sometimes taking three or four days. Because of that, their carriers couldn't make appointments to bring in containers or product on trailers because we were booked out two weeks in advance. And when he eventually did call back, he would complain about how he was slammed. The truth was he just didn't like dealing with them—he would spend half his time in the shipping and receiving area to avoid the customers.

After four days, customers' demerge charges would start, which could add up fast at $100.00 a day per container. That was why they needed their containers and trailers offloaded as soon as they arrive at their ports. But due to the operations manager's avoidance, we had to keep pushing out the appointments.

We were also running low on skilled manpower to drive forklifts and load slip sheets. Even with customers providing forecasts in advance, it didn't help because our company didn't want to hire additional forklift drivers.

Soon we had customers asking us to find them another 3PL warehouse where they could send their product without the constant headaches. That makes it tough on the Account Executive and on the CSRs, since our goal was to keep our customers happy and issue-free. I could feel a change coming and I needed to come up with plan B.

But fate had other plans.

The stress kept building up and it took its toll on my body, draining me mentally. Then one day I was taking a shower and felt something in my right breast. I was in complete denial, thinking it would go away, but no such luck. Finally I decided to get in to see my doctor and have a mammogram. The results came back—I did have a lump that showed on the mammogram. My world turned upside down. The flood of emotions just kept coming, and some days I felt as if I could not breath and that my heart would break.

The doctor scheduled an appointment for a biopsy and the tissue sample came back as fast-spreading cancer. They scheduled me for surgery the next week. I met with so many doctors in the next five days, giving me advice and options on what methods and treatments I should be using and how long I should be on chemo.

The surgery went well, and the surgeon felt she had gotten all of the cancer. Two weeks later I started chemo and lost all of my hair. And I do mean all—on my arms, my legs, my eyebrows, everywhere! Wigs became my best friend and I had lots of them, along with having my eyebrows tattooed with a beautiful arch. All of that made me feel so much better.

I kept working so as to keep my mind busy and to not dwell on my cancer. I only watched comedies on TV, and listened to audio on the best remedies and natural medicines to fight the disease. There were some great programs on YouTube with proven cases on how best to approach my type of breast cancer—you just have to be diligent to seek what methods are best for your body, your blood type and how far the cancer has traveled in your body.

It still wasn't smooth sailing. After my fourth chemo treatment, my teeth became loose, and by then I had lost 17 pounds. And starting three days after each treatment, I had to take shots every day for five days straight, one on the left side of my abdomen and one on the right side. They were very painful, leaving black-and-blue marks around the injection sites that made it look like I'd been beaten up by thugs.

I was in so much pain, it hurt to zip up my pants and wear underwear; plus I had no energy, and the chemo made my skin look gray and ashy—no matter how much makeup I put on, I looked like death warmed over.

One day during treatment, I noticed the lady across the room also taking her chemo with the same sized bag of chemicals (what they called "the red devil"), but she looked to be about 220 pounds to my 130 and falling. I said to myself, "Why is my bag the same size as hers?" And she wasn't feeling as sick as I was afterward, nor were her teeth coming loose.

I made an appointment with my oncologist to ask about this, and was shocked by her response: "I can cut it back by 25% if you want me to." That's when I knew I had to take total control of my treatment, including going to human resources and sharing with them what she'd said. The next thing I knew, I was assigned a new oncologist! When I asked what happened to the last one, no one would talk. (Later I found out later they'd moved her to another town, fearing a lawsuit.)

With a lower chemo dosage, I felt a lot better and my teeth started to heal. I would go to the hospital every Friday afternoon and sit in a warm chair for two hours while the chemo drip-fed into my arm and my blood stream. Then I would go home and crash until around noon the next day when I would wake up, eat, go to the bathroom and back to bed. By Sunday afternoon I started to feel halfway normal, and I could go back to work on Monday.

Most people didn't even know what I was going through, and I wanted to keep it that way. I stayed close to the customers, handled all the contracts, bid on new business and networked for new packaging business. My boss was understanding and kept my diagnosis a secret from the rest of the staff. Luckily I had a desk job, so I could save my energy. It was a blessing to work with the customers and walk the warehouse, as it helped take my mind off the pain and the next session of chemo.

During this time, we had a delegation of 27 people from several 3PL firms in Japan come by. They were visiting California to learn how logistics is run in the U.S. and to collaborate with us. I have several photos of me with the team from Japan and I enjoyed talking and sharing ideas and methods of logistics operations. They loved my blond hair and had no idea it wasn't real—not a hair on my head underneath those wigs. When I'd arrive home for the evening, I'd just wear a baseball cap to cover my bald head.

Once I completed all my chemo treatments, I put together a health program for myself, including meditation three times a day, a protein drink packed with all kinds of greens every morning, vitamins and herbal tinctures with healing properties. I started getting my energy back and my hair started growing again on my head.

I was looking forward to having a full head of hair one day—and to stop wearing wigs, as I'd had a couple of close calls with them. Once I received a hug and the bracelet on her wrist got caught in my wig—she kept pulling until I said, "Stop or you might see something funny." That's when I had to tell her I was wearing a rug—she was shocked! (I still have my wigs to this day, as a reminder that I can overcome anything and how far I've come in my journey.)

The best part about my treatments was the friends I made during my hospital visits. I did my best to encourage them to stay strong and keep their minds free from negative thinking. It's worth it to watch funny movies, keeping dressing in nice clothes and take your vitamins and protein drinks every day. To this day I tell everyone to turn off the news and turn on music—it is so good for the soul!

As of today I'm cancer free and all of my hair grew back except my eyebrows, legs and armpits.

Which is fine—it saves a lot of shaving, and my eyebrow tattoos save a lot of time in the morning when getting ready for the day.

Going through all that made me especially grateful for every day, for all of my friendships and what health I had left.

CHAPTER 18

Bouncing Back

Life doesn't stop just because you're sick. After cancer I kept up my protein shake and vitamins every morning and still do to this day. I kept working and enjoyed landing new accounts and all the emails and phone calls that go with being a saleswoman.

Business really started to pick up and a new warehousing and packaging opportunity came up for us, which needed all of my attention. Not only did it involve a demanding account, but there were many sides to this new business: shipping, targeted launch dates when introducing new items, getting pricing in a range that was acceptable and profitable for both parties, and building a long-term partnership that was key to making all of the rest happen.

They wanted us to use our company's shipping accounts, passing along our discounts to them. We'd tried that in the past with other customers and it had been a huge mistake, because you must pay your invoices weekly or they cut you off until you catch up. Those charges can add up fast, thousands of dollars a week. By the time we invoiced our customers at the end of the month they were into us for a bundle, including the markup for using our account number.

There are so many shipping companies out there that you can partner with and make a profit without breaking the bank. Keep in mind that in the U.S., shipping costs go by zip code, weight, zones and how often you ship to a particular location. The more you ship, the bigger the discounts, so you have to do your homework, get multiple quotes, try them out first on a trial basis, and don't sign a contract until they have proven themselves.

It can be hell to try to get out of a contract that you should have never signed in the first place, so don't sign anything until your lawyer or legal department reviews all the documents. And make sure to always have an out in case the shipping people don't fulfill their end of the bargain or deliver what they promised you.

Once we had all the pricing in place and had hired additional people to handle the new account, it was time to pull the trigger. We ended up having on average over 200 inbounds and 200 outbounds per day from them, but we pulled it off like a well-drilled combat unit. We had all the "soldiers" on the front line—guiding loads to the warehouse sections, moving product that needed packaging to the middle of the warehouse where production was located, getting all that merchandise on and off the trucks.

The line leads' offices all had glass windows so they could see the production going on. Should a line go down, a red light came on and everyone hurried to get that line going again ASAP. If they couldn't, the leads had to send the people home or find something else for them to do, because otherwise the company would be hemorrhaging dollars and have nothing to show for it.

You can't invoice downtime back to the customer, unless their product is what keeps jamming up your equipment and causing line downtime. In that situation, you'd better get on the phone with the customer and report it to them immediately, along with lots of photos as evidence. The clock is ticking, and someone has to pay for unproductive time on a production line—you don't want it to be you.

The best part about being in sales is that there is never a dull moment—although you do receive the strangest phone calls. During this period I got a call from someone in Europe saying they already had their product in two containers on a ship that would be landing at the Port of Oakland in four days, and they needed warehouse space! Talk about not planning ahead.

Well, a new customer is a new customer, so I sent him a profile to fill out and return back to me. When he did, I found out his product was rice, which presented a whole lot of extra problems—at the top of which was whether the rice fumigated before it left its port of call? (Raw grains can harbor all manner of nasty vermin that you don't want in your facility.) There were enough other questions in addition that, in the end, we turned this account away and told him to find another warehouse.

Several days later, the containers showed up at our warehouse without an appointment. We refused them, naturally, but then my phone and my email inbox lit up, with the guy from Europe telling me we have to receive the containers or else. Or else what? I told him all we ever did was talk and I never sent them a contract, never mind receiving a signed one back. He didn't have a leg to stand on, in America, Europe or anywhere else.

That was a lesson I'd already learned, thankfully: always make it clear that no product is to be shipped to your warehouse without a signed contract—period!

The adventures continued until 2020. Then COVID hit and things got seriously crazy. When the pandemic hit, it was a shock to the supply chain industry just as much as it was to every other field. I had to go into damage control mode and made sure I called every customer to let them know there would be no interruption of service—warehousing was absolutely an "essential business." In fact, I made it a practice to keep in touch with all our customers either by email or phone. I could tell in their voices how nervous they felt, wondering if their business would survive or how long the pandemic would last.

It took a toll on me because I'm a people person and was used to calling on my customers in person. That all stopped abruptly—now I had to change gears and become a therapist, listening to all the issues that COVID caused their employees, how many of their staff never came back to work or died due to underlying conditions.

We didn't have to close, but everyone in the business had to go into sanitation mode: washing hands all the time and wearing masks while we kept the product moving. Our operations manager did an excellent job keeping everyone masked up and six feet apart at all times. We had three people working full-time just wiping everything down with disinfectant—door handles, bathrooms and every part of the warehouse people touched. I would only go into the office to pick up samples and say hi to everyone, then be on my way.

We adjusted. Some 3PL firms didn't do so well and went out of business. The general public will never know all the sacrifices or the overtime we spent to keep food on their tables. We owe a great deal to all the supply chain warehouses throughout the U.S. and the world.

When we finally made it back to normal, about a year and a half later, we had all learned some harsh lessons about how many hands touch the food we eat before it reaches the stores. Not to mention how to deal with shortages—bottled water and toilet paper were gone from most shelves, and even when it did come back it was rationed. There were even people hoarding it or selling it on the Dark Web.

It was after that period that I started thinking seriously about writing this book and sharing my warehousing experiences with the world. I was also exhausted enough that I started thinking seriously about retiring

CHAPTER 19

Holding My Feet to the Fire, Literally, in Sales School

From the very start I always read books on sales and attended sales conferences and seminars. One of the best I attended was Tony Robbins' 7-day business and leadership conference in Los Angeles. I was given a gift from my dear friends Mike and JoAnne Gaffey at Gaffey & Associates—their daughter became pregnant and was unable to attend, so they offered me the conference. All I had to do was pay for my hotel room, food and air fare. What a deal!

I'd met JoAnne in the late '90s at my brother John's gym. When you meet someone who's going to be special in your life, that bond is instant and obvious—and we still have that bond to this day. JoAnne invited me to all her and her husband Mike's family holidays and get-togethers, and set a good example for David and I—my family had been so dysfunctional. Not that they were immune to family issues, but they knew better than I how to work through them.

It was good to have a friend I could talk to and run things by, to learn how to handle situations and weigh my options. Mike gave me good advice on business issues—he had his own business and understood what I was going through. They stood by my side, supported me with love and helped me stay grounded during difficult times. We are friends to this day and I love them both very much.

The first night of the Tony Robbins conference was the most intense—after class all day, we all made the "walk of fire" over hot coals at 1,200 degrees. Yes, I walked the fire, but only after a doctor fainted in front of me and was taken away on a stretcher with other doctors attending to him. I learned so much and still use many of Tony's lessons today, referring to the books and materials I received that week in L.A.

The Learning Annex in San Francisco is another great place to take courses in person and online for sales. Some of the other books I recommend:

- The 10X Rule: The Only Difference Between Success and Failure—Grant Cardone Secrets of Selling—Grant Cardone
- How to Be a Power Connector: The 5+50+100 Rule for Turning Your Business Network into Profits—Judy Robinett
- Selling in Manufacturing and Logistics: Take Control of the Selling Day—Norris Penha
- The Silva UltraMind series—Jose Silva and others
- Sandler Success Principles: 11 Insights that Will Change the Way You Think and Sell—Bruce Seidman, Sean Pratt, et al.
- Ditch The Pitch: The Art of Improvised Persuasion—Steve Yastrow
- Never Cold Call Again: Achieve Sales Greatness Without Cold Calling—Frank J. Rumbauskas

I read one book a week, sometimes two a week counting audiobooks. I can also suggest the podcast *Packaging Unboxd* with Evelio Mattos, which is all about packaging design.

Among the things I've learned that are basic to the selling life:

- Always be curious.

- Never stop learning.
- Be nice to everyone you meet, because everyone has a story to tell and they are dealing with family and work issues just like you.
- When you are in sales it's all about the customer.
- Never give advice—just listen, and most of the time they answer their own questions. They just need a person to hear them out.
- Never, never, *never* talk about bad about other companies or people—that will come back to bite you in the ass.
- Hold your head up high.
- Know that when you work in logistics you are supplying food to the nations, so humble yourself.

And you if do it right, you will never be out of a job or go hungry!

After the sale, after the contract has been signed and executed, is when the rubber really meets the road. Now you need to set up the new items in the system, and assign a customer service rep that will be a good fit for this customer and will communicate and keep them happy. On a few occasions I had to change CSRs on a new customer because it was just not a good fit, or there were personality issues. Better to make the change fast and do not delay as the customer is paying the bills and you will require less recovery time.

Personalities are so important in this business. I should have a sign on my door that says Account Executive, Sales and Therapist. Some of the most successful people I have met are so unhappy, and when you are in sales, again, it's all about the customer. I could almost have a degree as a psychiatrist by now from all the stories I have heard.

After I sign up a new customer, I will have a Zoom or conference call to introduce them to the team and share all the contact information—e-mails and phone numbers, including the Operations

Manager's direct line and private cell number and an after-hours emergency phone number. I'll also send them a welcome package with wine and chocolate and a nice card, just like my Dad did.

With a new customer, for the first two to three months I make sure I'm copied on all emails, including the transportation emails. You want the customer to be able to make one call for all of your services—warehousing, transportation, packaging, whatever—so they can concentrate on selling their product and building a bigger customer base. And when they call me, I need to have all the information at my fingertips. Everyone wins and our customers love us.

Also, when you sign up a new customer don't forget to request monthly and yearly forecasts so you know how to plan your warehouse space and labor. If they only want to warehouse for six months, say, then the rates will be much higher unless you backfill with another customer for the time that space is empty. It's always a balancing act and the goal is to keep the warehouse racks and bulk area full year-round.

Now when it comes to turns, you want their product to move every month—that's how you make your money. If it just sits there and only moves once or twice a year, the warehousing pricing per pallet must be higher. Again, that is why you need that forecast from the customer when you onboard them. Plus, the forecast will tell you if they have big pushes during the holidays or other times of the year you need to plan labor for. The only exception is if it's a new product and has no history of sales records; then you must be on the phone with them or they must keep you updated every month.

And then you get the new customers that have deep pockets and start out small, then they have big product launches and it blows up in your face—you run out of space and need to acquire additional warehouse space, equipment and employees fast. I have seen that happen on at least three occasions, and in all three cases a bigger company bought them out. Not every customer is prepared to handle success.

Nor is every customer prepared for failure. Always, and I mean *always*, be very careful when a new customer puts a lot of pressure on you to move all their product into your warehouse in a week or less. That should be a red flag from the very start.

I remember one customer where my gut feeling was telling me something was not right. Then when the first truckload came in, the product didn't look right and had a slight musty smell to it. Later that afternoon as I was taking my walk I looked at the product again and could see tiny bugs under the shrink wrap. Red alert!

I got the receiving manager on the phone, then called our QC dept and told them to get out to the warehouse by doors 70 and 71 and to bring the black light. Sure enough, we found more bugs, not to mention mouse poop and urine. I put out a 911 to our pest control company so they could get the product on one of their trailers and get it off the property.

It was just in time too, as we had seven more trucks on the books for the next day's inbound. Needless to say, I told shipping and receiving to cancel all inbounds for this customer. Next I called and sent an email to the new customer with all the photos of the bugs and told them no more inbounds until we inspected the product at the warehouse it was being sent from. That didn't happen, as they would not allow us on their property or warehouse, period. Plus it was end of month and they wanted all this done in the next five days—very suspicious. I finally had to tell the new customer we could not receive any more of their product and sent them on their way.

Later I found out they had to dump all of their product at the local landfill and take a high loss. Had we not found the bugs on the first load we would have had a nightmare on our hands and it would have infested our other customers' product.

That's why you should always listen to your gut—and have any new customer send you photos of their product, give you the all the information about where the product is coming from and check the first load, no exceptions. Your five senses, not to mention your instincts, need to be in operation at any warehouse.

One other tip: always have two new customers in your back pocket at all times to fill that warehouse space, so you're not sucking air and have a big layoff if a current customer pulls out (or has to be sent off). Everything depends on your sales skills, on staying positive and supporting your team at all times. You have employees for years and need to do everything to keep them on the payroll until you get over the hump and back to normal. They are the backbone of your organization.

CHAPTER 20

Team Play

Your team is everything and you must empower them at all times! They take care of the customers on all levels whether you're in the office or away traveling to food shows or on the road doing cold calls.

When at the food shows I would always bring back free samples and nice gifts for all the office and warehouse personnel. I'd also take a lot of photos of our customers' booths at the food shows to promote the partnership with our team. Customers loved for me to take messages back to the teammates who oversaw their accounts, and to send gifts back with me too.

On my walks through the office, warehouse or production I would always have conversations with my teammates and tell them how proud I was of them and what a great job they were all doing. Because of this, they felt comfortable enough to air their differences with me without judgment. They would also share ideas on how to trim expenses and save money. Not only are we teammates, we are family and we need to support each other at all times.

Every month we would have a lunch—pizza, sub sandwiches, burgers or whatever—just to say what a great job the team was doing and that management appreciated all their hard work. I would send them note cards letting them know how special they were to the team.

We need to empower and encourage our younger generation to take care of the next generation of employees and their families as well. We are all connected on every level, and food is something we can't live without. Knowing where your food comes from and how it's handled is of high importance. We need to get back to the basics and get away from all the GMOs and additives and pesticides we put in or on our foods.

And your team isn't just the people in your office or on your production floor—it's also the folks behind the wheel of your (or your business partner's) big rigs. Almost every eighteen-wheeler you see on the road is either picking up or dropping off a load of food to a major distribution center, club store, retailer or manufacturer. It's up to the carriers, the trucking companies, to make sure what they carry is delivered on time and in good condition, with every pallet intact and nothing going missing in between stops. And most of that responsibility falls on the truck drivers.

Drivers have to be bookkeepers, master negotiators, and detectives, reading between the lines as to who is telling the truth and who's fibbing. They also must be good at smooth-talking the next appointment clerk because they're running late to their appointment, due to the last place they stopped taking forever to unload because the forklift driver was newly-trained, had never unloaded a live load, and was nervous as hell about dropping a pallet or driving the forks through the product.

When you're a truck driver, you learn quickly that rudeness gets you nowhere fast. It's always better to be nice to the shipping and receiving personnel. If you're kind, keep your cool and tell them what a great job they are doing, odds are you will make a friend for life.

With all the shipping and receiving personnel that I have met, behind and in front of their check-in windows, the kinder you are to them, the faster the service you will receive. They will usually arrange workarounds if you're running late or get stuck in traffic—provided you call ahead, give them a heads-up that you're on your way and give them an ETA. That way you can know if they are going to wait for you, and if there are extra charges you will need to pay because you have extended the team into overtime.

If you call too late and everyone has gone home for the day ... well, you're likely SOL and will have to schedule a new appointment. That won't make your dispatcher very happy. It also won't make you happy, because you've just wasted diesel fuel and time on the road, which cuts into your profits. Needless to say, your customer won't be please that their product didn't make it in time, especially in cases where it needs to be consolidated with other product that night at the DC and shipped out to a customer the next morning.

Today everyone wants what they ordered the same day or the next day, with no excuses and no no extra charges. Of course that means *someone* has to pay the late charges and rescheduling fees, and that most often falls on the carrier or an independent driver, or billed back to the original customer. In some circumstances it's better to walk away and not get caught up in that thankless merry-go-round. As a drive, you need to find an employer with which you're happy, a carrier that appreciates your hard work and can-do attitude.

And did I mention the long hours on the road, missing your family members and special events like birthday parties? If you like being home at night, then sign with a local carrier. But if you like the open road and adventure, then go with a long-haul company. You'll get to see the whole U.S.A. and meet interesting people. But keep in mind that you'll need to know all the traffic laws in all the states (and provinces) you drive through. And some of the small towns have their own traffic laws, if you know what I mean.

Once we had one of our out-of-state drivers take a full truckload (FTL) up north. He parked his tractor-trailer in an empty parking lot with no tow signs of any kind. But around two in the morning he got a knock on his window from the town sheriff, who told our driver that he needed to get out of his sleepover cab, and go to a hotel in town and get a room.

Our driver was like, "What the hell are you talking about? I'm sleeping just fine in my cab." The sheriff informed him the town had a no-cab-sleepover ordinance, because they were trying to generate revenue for their small town. If the driver didn't get a room in town immediately, they would tow his tractor-trailer and impound it until he paid the fees to get it back—around $1,500 plus $200 a day for storage. Keep in mind our driver could only work so many hours a day by law, and he'd run out—he *had* to spend the night there.

The sheriff was kind enough to give our driver a ride to the local hotel that night, and in the morning he got a ride back to his truck where he'd parked it the day before. No issues. Everyone was happy

Another time I had a driver whom I needed to park their truck in a fenced-in yard because the batteries were exposed on the outside of the trailer. The problem was that the yard was all locked up by the time the driver got there. I reached out to the head honcho there, but when I didn't get an answer in time, we had to park the tractor-trailer overnight in front of a house. When the driver woke up in the morning, all three of the batteries had been stolen! We found out later that some of the local homeless population had stolen them to cook their food, run TVs and charge their phones. Clever on the part of the homeless, but it left our driver in quite a bind.

So if you're driving a big rig, always check with the small towns where you plan on spending a night to make sure there are no laws that forbid you from parking your tractor sleepover cab—or any other sneaky laws you might not know about. And look around where you stop—because local laws aren't the only things that can get you.

CHAPTER 21

More than Lipstick on a Pig: Logistics Lessons

I have always said that if you give excellent service, provide a fair price, deliver what you say you're going to do and on time every time, you will keep your customers happy and you will have a customer and a partnership for a lifetime. In addition, I have a few rules:

1. Always return a call, text or e-mail within 30 minutes after you receive it unless it's after work or on a weekend. And even then I still return calls as soon as I can, no matter what.
2. Keep your current customers happy and your CSRs well paid and you will never be at a loss for business. Repeat business is the goal.
3. Always have at least two new customers in your back pocket to back fill the warehouse/packaging just in case a customer leaves.
4. Technology—WMS and the IT department must make ongoing improvements at all times.
5. Keep your employees paid well, always treat them with respect and let them know that you appreciate them at all times.

One lesson I learned the hard way was how to stay in my lane and not do other people's jobs. Once I talked back to the Vice President of Operations, and when I was about to go home he told me to come to work the next morning dressed in jeans and work boots because I would be working the production line the next day and he would hold all my calls until he felt I learned my lesson. The reason he was so upset is that production was his wheelhouse and mine was sales. That lasted only one day. Within the week, he came back to me and asked for the information on an equipment company I had found online and that I interviewed, it turns out he ended up using that company I did all the research on.

By the way, I had fun that day in production and had everyone singing with the music turned up loud. We had a good laugh later when we all went out for pizza after work.

But as the sales person, I had more than enough to do. I was attending all the food, candy and packaging shows like the Fancy Food show in San Francisco, Expo West in Los Angeles and the Packaging Expo in Chicago, not to mention spending a lot of time on the road visiting customers to make sure they were happy with our 3PL services. Going out to dinner with customers I especially enjoyed.

Every Christmas the owner would ship out high-end bottles of wine and candy to every customer, or hand-deliver them if we were close by. Christmas cards were a favorite part of my job—we all hand-signed every card and I would address each card by hand to give it that personal touch. Christmas was also a good time to smooth over a misshipment or sit and listen to whatever complaints a customer had. You knew you had better get back to them with a corrective action plan if you wanted to keep their business.

Interpersonal relationships are a huge—and underrated—factor in gaining and keeping a customer's business. When setting up a new customer, be very mindful of the CSR you assign to them. Make sure your CSR is compatible with the new customer and has a pleasant personality. You'll want someone with a can-do attitude, who has the vision to read between the lines, a clear understanding and knowledge of the customer's products and an extensive knowledge of how to handle those products.

For instance, canned soup and tomatoes always need to be stored in a well, in racks, or 2-3 high bulk stacks with good visibility. Make sure you have a good sniffer, because if a can leaks they can go bad fast and the smell is overwhelming—it will penetrate other products stored right next to it, especially things like boxed crackers, wrapped candy and chips.

Think of it like the warehouse is your home during the day, and treat it as you would treat your home when you get off work. You want to arrive at home with clean carpets, fresh smelling air, dishes washed and put away, and the counter tops clean and free of clutter.

Once I went to visit another warehouse because we needed short-term space for a customer. When I entered it, the smell was overpowering, like someone had opened the world's largest can of rotten cat food. The aisles were full of garbage, paper wrappings, stretch wrap from pallets and old cardboard boxes. And they were AIB certified! I was in shock—there was no way I was putting my customer's product in that disgusting operation. (Not to mention they wanted way too much for storage and handling.) I left as soon as I could and never looked back. It took several visits to other 3PL warehouses in the area before I found an operation that I trusted and that would sign a non-disclosure agreement (because we didn't want them to steal our customer).

It's also important to get an extensive customer profile, having them fill it out and provide a forecast, make a credit check and obtain three valid references before they bring a single box of product into your warehouse. (See the samples of a customer profile and a credit application following this chapter.) You must do your due diligence and find out why they want to leave their current warehouse. Is it because they raised their prices, or are always damaging or misplacing product? Or is it because they aren't paying their bills and were given a thirty-day notice to leave? If they are not transparent or if you feel like they're hiding something, follow your gut and run from that account as fast as you can.

A new account is in general a blessing—it means you will have money coming in every month as long as you don't screw it up. So, congratulations! But there are a lot of details you need to watch when you set it up:

- How many pallets will you be warehousing?
- How high will the pallets be stacked—one, two, three high or bulk stack?
- How many racks or how big a bulk stack area will you need?
- Are there any food allergen issues?
- Does the product need to be kept dry, frozen or at a certain temperature?
- Who will be the customer service representative?
- How does the customer want their product tracked and shipped out—by lot code, BBD or FIFO?
- What is the shelf life of the product?

You'll need your IT person or CSR supervisor to set all this up correctly in your system, and to give your new customer a login and password so they can access your system and see their inventory 24/7. Also, your customer will need an emergency contact person's name and after-hours phone number and text number.

Now if you have an account that's always late on paying their invoices, help them find another warehouse and give them a good reference, then count your blessings and trust a new account will come your way very soon. It's always been that way for me, and if you have a good reputation on the street, you will always have a full warehouse with customers who pay on time.

If you run a good 3PL company, keep an eye on your profits and losses, and have a team that's got your back, you can make a very good living and have great friends too. Once that new customer signs the contract, you have a partnership, and if it's working well they will tell ten other people, which brings in more business and lifelong customers.

When you open the doors to a new warehouse, you need to be everything to your incoming customers. Some warehouse seekers are pros when looking for the right fit for their product and some are not, but either way you must hold their hand and show them the ropes.

Ask a lot of questions and send them a customer profile to be filled out and returned to you so you have a good idea of what you're dealing with, plus a forecast for the next year. (See Chapter 17 for a sample customer profile.) You definitely need to know how many times a product turns over every month or if it only moves three or four times a year. Let's face it, you don't make money on product that just sits or barely moves. And if it just sits, the storage rate goes up—if it moves every month, that helps the rate come down.

If your potential customers are pros, they will ask for all of your documentation from the very moment they enter the warehouse. If you don't have your paperwork in order, it will kill the deal for sure! You must have all of your certificates on display and have copies ready to be sent electronically to your new customers.

They'll also want to see all of the pest control reports from the last year, and to make sure you don't have a bug problem. Once we had a new flour customer and they were putting a lot of pressure on us to move all of their five-pound flour bags into our warehouse. "Not so fast—we need to see the product first! Let's move a few loads over and do an QC check." Sure enough, the flour bags had bugs inside *and* outside. No way were we about to warehouse that—it would have spread bugs into other customers' product throughout the warehouse. We avoided a catastrophe.

Next, you need to have the Warehouse Services Procedures and Protocols written out, give them a copy, have them read it and agree, then sign and date the document. Give them a copy and you keep the original in your files so there are no surprises—or lawsuits.

Customer Profile

Account Name	
Completed by	

STORAGE CHARACTERISTICS

Days and Hours of Operation	
Desired location for warehouse	

If item/SKU detail is available, please attach (carton dimensions, eaches per case, cases per pallet, weight, pallet dimensions)

Product Description			
Total Square Feet		Racking %	
Temperature Requirement		Bulk %	
Total Stock Keeping Units		Bulk Stack Height	
Average Pallets on hand per month		Lot Controlled	
Average Cases on hand per month		Serial Number Tracking	
Average Cases per pallet		Expiration Date Tracking	
Estimated Inventory Turns		Rotation Required	
Case Weight (lbs.)		Pallet Size(s) (LxWxH, inches)	
Average Case Dimensions (inches)		Pallet Weight (lbs.)	

Comments:

INBOUND CHARACTERISTICS

Annual Receipts / Inbounds		Average Line Items per	
Monthly Receipts / Inbounds		Average Pallets per load	
Annual Pallets Received		Average Units per load	
Annual Cases Received		Unload Type:	

Receipt Type:		% Mixed Pallet	
% Full Truck		% Palletized	
% LTL		% Floorloaded	
% Container		% Slipsheet	
% Rail		% Clamp	
% Other		% Other	
Comments:			

OUTBOUND CHARACTERISTICS

Breakout orders by shipment type if applicable below

Annual Orders		Average Lines per order	
Average Orders per day		Average Pallets per order	
Annual Pallets Shipped		Average Units per order	
Annual Units Shipped		Order Unit Pick	
Shipment Type:		% Pallet Pick	
% Full Truck		% Case Pick	
% LTL		% Each Pick	
% Small Parcel		Order Turnaround:	
% Other (describe in		% Same Day	
Repack %		% Next Day	
Seasonality		% Future Days	
Comments:			

Account Name	

RECEIPT AND ORDER PROCESSING – SPECIAL SERVICES

Receipt Advance Arrival		Consignee Information:	
Orders Received		Retail %	

Routing		E-Commerce %		
Labeling (Type)		Drop Ship %		
Retail Compliance		Distributors / Wholesalers		
Cycle Count Requirement		Other %		
Other Special Services		Top 3 Consignees:		

Comments: _____

_____

ORDER PROFILE DETAILED BREAKDOWN

	Truckload	LTL	Parcel / Small Package
Annual Orders			
Average Orders per day			
Annual Pallets Shipped			
Annual Units Shipped			
Average Line Items per order			
Average Pallets per order			
Average Units per order			
Order Unit Pick			
% Pallet Pick			
% Case Pick			
% Each Pick			
Shipment Type:			
% Full Truck			
% LTL			
% Small Parcel			
% Other (describe in			
% Same Day			

% Next Day				
% Future Days				
Repack %				
Top Carriers				

OTHER INFORMATION

Account Name

CONTACT INFORMATION

Information needed for main contact and verifying company

Contact Name

Title

Company Name

Address

City, State, Zip

Phone	( )
E-mail	
Name of Business Owner	
Type of Business to Outsource	[ ] Warehouse
	[ ] Transportation
	[ ] Both
Estimated Annual Revenue	
D&B #	
Planned Start Date	

CREDIT APPLICATION

NAME _____

ADDRESS _____

CITY _____ STATE _____ ZIP _____

BILLING ADDRESS _____

CITY _____ STATE _____ ZIP _____

PHONE _____ CONTACT _____

OWNER(S) _____

YEARS IN OPERATION _____ APPLYING FOR CREDIT AMOUNT _____

BANK NAME _____ # OF YEARS WITH BANK _____

BANK ADDRESS _____

CITY _____ STATE _____ ZIP _____

PHONE _____ CONTACT _____

ACCOUNT NUMBER _____

REFERENCE 1 – NAME _____

PHONE _____ FAX _____

ADDRESS _____ CITY _____ STATE _____ ZIP _____

REFERENCE 2 – NAME _____

PHONE _____ FAX _____

ADDRESS _____ CITY _____ STATE _____ ZIP _____

REFERENCE 3 – NAME _____

PHONE _____ FAX _____

ADDRESS _____ CITY _____ STATE _____ ZIP _____

CHAPTER 22

Insurance and Other Things to Watch For

When looking for a warehouse, you want to make sure your product has coverage under their insurance policy and/or you have you own coverage. Read the contract very carefully before you sign, make sure you have your attorney read it and ask any questions up front, and put it all in writing (or at least an email) so you have a paper trail. Some customers self-insure their product in exchange for lower storage and handing rates. Ask for a copy of their insurance policy and see how much coverage they carry. If they need more insurance on their product, they will have to pay more in warehouse rates.

Before you move your product in, you need to find out exactly how much insurance coverage they have, what is the deductible, have they ever had a claim, and if so, how much was the claim. Don't be afraid to ask for a copy of their insurance either—you have to be sure they'll back up their promises, because you never know what might happen.

At one warehouse, we had one of the riser water pipes on the ceiling break and it flooded the whole west end of the building. We received a notice at 2:00 a.m. from the fire department that the water pressure had fallen—that will make your heart stop! The operation manager drove up to the warehouse and saw water rushing out of about twenty of the closed roll-up doors, some of which the water pressure had knocked off their tracks. There was such massive flooding that the fire crews had to shut off the water at the main valve.

When we finally entered the warehouse, there was still three feet of water on the floor, though it was draining out rapidly. Boxes, cases, half-full pallets and all kinds of material were floating by us, all waterlogged. That's when you realize the power of water and the damage it can cause. When all was said and done, insurance had to cover over a million dollars in damages, and the amount of water-damaged product we had to take the dump was off the charts.

It took two crews of twenty to push out all the water with huge squeeze mops from the local hardware stores. The water department came out the next day and wanted to know what the hell was going on, so we took them on a tour of the warehouse and their jaws dropped— they had never seen anything like it.

We ended up suing the piping company that built the fire riser system on the building. We won the case and were reimbursed all damages, including for the ruined product. We only lost one customer because of the water accident, and that one was understandable, as their product was high-end: yeast that goes into wine tanks at just the right time when making wine. It's critical that the yeast is added in a very specific 10-12 hour period, or the whole batch goes bad, a total loss. The cost of that yeast is about $1,200 per case wholesale.

A lot of the product could be repacked and salvaged into new boxes, including canned goods and bagged food that had no water damage inside, stuff where only the outside case got wet.

Another time we had chips that were very spicy and the smell leaked into some expensive coffee. All of a sudden our customer started receiving complaints that the coffee tasted funny, and they wanted to know what part of the warehouse we were storing it in. We immediately moved the coffee into another section of the warehouse so that we could air out, and in a few days the smell disappeared. It's hugely important to keep your nose (and other senses) on high alert when walking in the warehouse.

(That's also why I would never want a bathroom next to my kitchen or dining room. Better to keep it on the other side of the house.)

It's still automatic for my five senses to come to life every time I walk into a warehouse. My sense of smell will tell if any product has been spoiled or has been spilled because the pallets will pick up the odor and continue to give it off until you dump the pallets or dump the product. Sometimes you have to dump everything, including the mops and rags used to clean up the mess.

As far as sight, it's natural for me to look for pallets that are leaning, or product on broken pallets that are ready to fall over and come crashing to the floor—or worse, on warehouse personnel.

Hearing is a big one—your ears must be honed to all the sounds in the warehouse. Once I stopped walking because I kept hearing this little squeak from the rafters. Turns out a bird had built a nest up near the skylight. Our QC department had a fit and had it removed the next day.

On several occasions, we had customers request that we do taste-testing for them. That can be fun with the right product—say, cookies covered in chocolate, or whiskey, or miniature chocolate-covered strawberries.

Touch is an underrated one. On one of my walks I noticed these tomato cans that looked like they were getting bigger. I was thinking it was just me until I had the shrink wrap removed from the pallets and found the cans *were* swelling and warm to the touch. Bacteria was growing inside the cans—yuck! QC was called and we had to put all the product on hold for the lot code batch. Eventually sixteen pallets of the stuff had to be dumped at the local landfill, all kinds of paperwork had to be filled out, and QC from the tomato company came out to take samples from the cans and do all kinds of documentation.

There are so many other things to watch out for in looking at a new warehouse. Do they have a backup generator in case the electricity goes out—not just to keep the air conditioning, heating and refrigeration on but also to run their computers and print out BOLs for outgoing orders? Where is the nearest fire department? How many miles away is it? And what is its response time to the location? Likewise the nearest hospital, and how well equipped are they to handle emergencies like heart attacks or broken legs and arms? Do they have an active shooter escape plan (you'll want to see the written plans)? How many warehouse personnel have been trained to handle a firearm, and how many carry a weapon with them to take out an active shooter? How many eye wash stations so they have in case someone gets a foreign substance in their eyes, and is there a map of their locations in the warehouse? And what if …?

Well, if you want any more tips, you'll have to retain my services at Truth About Logistics. I can't afford to give away all my expertise for free.

CHAPTER 23

Equipment and Other Dangers

There are gas-powered and battery-powered forklifts, but regardless of what kind they are, no matter how long you have been driving forklifts, you are open to accidents. You need to be on high alert at all times whenoperating one because you never know when you'll encounter an obstacle or a worker stepping out from behind a stack of pallets.

Once we had a twenty-plus-year forklift veteran drive right off the dock because he forgot to check the trailer wheels to make sure they were chucked. They weren't, and as he started to load the trailer the forklift shot off the dock, went airborne and landed on the pavement below. The driver hit the ground with such force it knocked the air out of him and he could not talk for about ten minutes.

We had to call an ambulance and have him transported to the hospital. He had six broken ribs, a fractured shoulder and a big cut on top of his head which required stitches. He was drug tested and they found no signs of drugs—he was just plane not paying attention! He was off work for six weeks, and when he did come back he was not only put on light duty but was required to undergo forklift training and testing all over again.

We had another forklift driver center-slam a major support beam, causing the whole building to shake like it was in an earthquake, and the sound was like a bomb went off—almost a sonic boom. Everyone came running out from the office only to see blood gushing out of the middle of his forehead—his head had struck the center pole when was thrown from the forklift, because he wasn't wearing his seat belt. That will get your attention real fast and leave a lasting impression.

Thankfully the building was empty and no pallets or product had been shipped in yet—they were still painting the lines down the aisles and installing racks to get the warehouse ready to receive product. Still trying to figure out how the driver managed to screw up that badly.

And once a 20-year forklift veteran drove off the dock with a full pallet of sugar in a 2,200-pound tote. The trailer driver had forgotten to put chucks under his tires so when our forklift driver pulled forward, the trailer pulled away from the dock. Our man's forehead was split down the middle and he too had to go the hospital and be stitched up. A few days later he came back to work with two of the biggest black eyes I have ever seen in my life. By the way, he passed his drug test and no disciplinary action was taken. Just the look of his face was enough of a reminder to everyone of what happens when someone doesn't follow the rules or check to make sure the trailer wheels are chucked.

Aside from operator error, forklift maintenance is a must. You need to have a PM (preventative maintenance) program in place so your forklifts are in top running condition at all times, and you need to provide ongoing training for all of your forklift drivers.

Likewise, drug testing and screening is critical in a warehouse. You are dealing with 9,000-pound forklifts and other heavy equipment, not to mention packaging equipment running on the warehouse floor with conveyor belts and bundle wrappers.

Once we had a line lead bend down and go under a conveyor belt to save time and unjam a line on the other side. There was no guard covering the belt, and she had long hair. The conveyor belt grabbed hold of her hair and dragged her over fifteen feet and then came to a turn, effectively scalping her—ripped the flesh right off the top of her head! The entire production team was in shock, and many of the workers fainted or got violently ill, as they'd never witnessed anything like that in their lives.

We called 911 and the paramedics, the fire department and an ambulance were there in under three minutes. They were all in shock too, and took immediate action to stop the bleeding and rush her to the hospital. A nurse tried to see if any of the scalp could be saved, but it was all in chunks—the belt and gears had chewed it up.

The next day Occupational Safety and Health officials were on site, and production was shut down until we could cover all the belts and install warning signs on all the lines. Then we had to schedule another OSHA visit so they could sign off on the improvements and give us written permission to start up production again. The company was fined $10,000.

As for the line lead, she had sixteen operations, in one of which they had to place an expandable balloon under her scalp to help grow new skin over her skull. She had to wear a protective helmet to cover her head, and was on strong painkillers for a long time due to ongoing headaches. She sued the company and won over $300,000, plus insurance for life to cover any medical expenses related to the scalp injury.

Needless to say, no one ever crawled under a conveyor belt again.

Equipment—and not respecting it—isn't the only hazard to life and limb in a warehouse. At one place where we warehoused a lot of chocolate, we had to have a very robust pest control program or we would have all kinds of insects, mice, rats and other vermin in our warehouse. Every week we would have to dump two or three pallets of damaged chocolate just from inbound trucks that had broken cases or melted product due to the refrigeration unit on the front of the trailer running out of diesel fuel.

Once we were doing a large rework project on a chocolate account, which meant a lot of the chocolate had to be thrown out. We had cameras on our dumpster to make sure no one went dumpster diving and took the chocolate to sell or give to their family. There were signs posted all around the dumpster not to take anything out of them, and during employee orientation everyone we hired had to sign and date a document stating you would not remove or take anything off the property without written permission from your supervisor.

Our operations manager caught one of our production people on the surveillance cameras stealing something like thirty cases of chocolate and filling the trunk of his car with it. What he didn't realize—though he should have; it was common knowledge—was that all food products that went into the dumpsters were sprayed with poison the same day. That was to keep all the ants and mice from invading our dumpsters and getting from them into the warehouse.

The next morning, we brought in the production worker in for questioning and he swore up and down that he did not steal any chocolate. Even when we showed him the footage from the camera with him stealing it, he still tried to deny it.

We left him in the conference room to cool his heels and think about what he'd done and how he wanted to handle it. While he was in there, he received a call from his wife, saying that she had to rush their daughter to the emergency room because she was throwing up blood and going into a coma. You guessed it—the idiot had not only stolen the chocolate, he'd let his six-year-old daughter have some of it. He came out of the conference room screaming and crying, saying he had to get to hospital and that his daughter was in grave danger.

He was fired on the spot, because he knew the rules and had signed the document (he wouldn't have been hired if he hadn't). And not only did he nearly lose his daughter because he'd stolen poised chocolate, but having lost his job meant he had no insurance and all of the poor girl's medical bills had to be paid out of pocket. All for a few "free" boxes of sweets.

Even in the best of circumstances, you never know what you're putting in your body, and you certainly don't know what you're putting in your body when it comes from a dumpster. Some people just don't have common sense, and because of that they put themselves and their family in harm's way. You can't make this stuff up.

CHAPTER 24

Time for a Change

Pre- and post-COVID was a trying, tiring time. The logistics market got soft as major manufacturers took their warehousing in-house to save money and manage their inventory more closely. It's a cycle the industry goes through every so often. Saving money on outside warehousing can be helpful in the short term, but the downside is that manufacturers soon find they can't deliver their goods in time to make the delivery dates on purchase orders, so they lose sales. And Heaven forbid their transportation company has a delay for whatever reason—the weather, over-the-road breakdowns, faulty equipment. One hiccup can bring your business to its knees fast.

This goes on all the time. Some manufacturers like to keep their products close to their customers for quick turnaround, because they have the margins to absorb the cost of warehousing their own product. But a lot of them can't pull it off.

On several occasions a company I worked for had a major client pull all their product out of our warehouses because a new CEO wanted to make his bottom-line numbers look good ... only to lose a lot of business because they couldn't deliver the product in time. Most companies don't keep large amounts of inventory on hand unless they have good margins and the product turns over fast and in volume. That's why they need third-party logistics firms like the ones I've worked for—3PLs have the capacity and expertise most manufacturers don't.

The companies who pull out tend to learn quickly that it pays to keep your product in outside warehouses in order to keep their customers happy and their orders filled promptly. It's all about how fast they receive our product once they place an order—we are a society that wants it NOW, and will pay a premium to get it! The companies that don't grasp that, or don't grasp it fast enough, don't last long.

That's when I thought about retiring and writing my book, so I left my last place of work. I felt like I was ready for the time off.

I have always kept notebooks on every person I spoke to—even the rude and shameful ones—events I attended, problems I faced. It's a habit I still practice to this day, and it has saved my bacon more times than I can count. I started going through all those notebooks from day one.

I had plenty of other things to occupy my time too. I enjoyed weekend trips to Napa Valley wine country and anyplace where they made or served champagne—northern California has loads of them. I went to Carmel, one of my favorite places in the world, to check out, put my feet in the Pacific Ocean and enjoy the fabulous weather and food. I did my Pilates and lots of walking every day and read my minimum of two books a week about the latest sales programs, management, companies going lean or going green with recycling programs, WMS systems, AI technology, health and self-love. I was a speaker at many women's events.

And after about three months I was going crazy. I started getting antsy and realized how much I missed being in a 3PL warehouse, in a family environment, working with passionate people that truly care about their customers and not treating them like a resource for their own gain.

But while I'd had a lot of job offers in those few months, nothing had excited me. On the other hand, retirement clearly wasn't exciting me either. What to do?

With all the flux in the industry, I got an idea. I had so many contacts in the warehousing world across the United States—why not start my own consulting business to help manufacturers select proven, reliable 3PL solutions for their product? Having been in this business for decades, I was sure I could go to work for myself. I couldn't possibly be worse as my own boss than some of the bosses I've had, after all. It was either that or retire for good.

Then a very good friend of mine, Chris Murphy, the CEO, and Abigail Power, Sales and Marketing, at of Sierra Pacific Warehouse Group, heard that I was striking out on my own. We connected and discussed me working for him and his beautiful daughter Abigail Power (she runs sales and marketing for SPWG) as a consultant for warehousing and packaging development.

I also shared with Chris Murphy that I was writing this book about my experiences as a woman in the logistics world from the early 1990s to today—I figured he deserved fair warning. But Chris said, "We support you, Judy, one hundred percent!"

I started in 2022 as a consultant with SPWG and soon added other customers as well. I put together programs such as twice-annual customer surveys and waste management to recycle fiber, shrink wrap, and banding so no more waste is sent to landfills. SPWG now does yearly audits on all its accounts, is building a robust packaging division for all its club store accounts, is building displays for retail and so much more.

I'm very grateful and honored to be working for Chris and Abigail, SPWG has been family-owned and operated since 1988. They're on their third generation, and the fourth is on its way as of this writing. It takes a special kind of organization and leader to see all of their people's talents and allow them to combine to be used for the good of the whole team. And it's a win-win for the customers too.

My life really is wonderful and satisfying. I get to work with SPWG and many other amazing companies as a consultant. I have enough free time to make short weekend trips to the Napa Valley, Monterey Bay and the Sierra Nevada Mountains. I enjoy spending time with my grandsons, watching them grow up to be fine, reasonable young men. I still exercise on my Pilates machine and make my protein drinks every morning, balanced by the occasional bottle of champagne. I attend concerts and other get-togethers or go to lunch or dinner with my girlfriends. And I'm grateful for every day!

I'm not the only one who's thriving. My wonderful son David is now married to a beautiful woman and they have two boys. My grandsons are amazing and so smart and loving—they are very mechanically inclined, computer wizards who can work on and fix anything. I am so proud of my son, as he stood by my side during our most difficult times.

David worked for both me and his dad to make extra money during summer months in high school and college—driving a forklift, pulling orders or building racks in a warehouse. It really paid off, as he already had the skills and experience that logistics people look for, while most college students that apply for jobs in the industry are book smart but not aware of how to run operations or manage inventories. David has worked for a major food service company for over fifteen years, ever since he graduated. I guess warehousing and logistics are in our DNA

There's a saying that if you work in the food business, you will never go hungry. There will always be a job for you and food on the table. I'm glad to see more high schools offering warehousing classes for senior-year students to introduce them to the warehousing business, give them credits and allow them to get experience under their belt. If you know how to count product and read lot codes and best-by dates, you are on your way to understanding how warehouses work and run.

Warehousing is to me the most rewarding career I could imagine.

Every day is different and challenging, and it's never boring. What a life I have had thanks to the wonderful people I've met in my thirty-plus years in the industry. And yes, there have also been some not-so-nice ones too, but you learn pretty quickly who your true friends are and who you can trust in the business. Writing this book has been very gratifying as well, knowing that I have a voice and that people

can learn how a warehouse works—but without those decades in the business, I'd have nothing to write.

Retire? Nope—I tried that. Now I'm unretired and having too much fun to stop. I plan on staying in the warehouse business for a very long time.

Acknowledgments

I am so grateful for my son David, who stood by my side during all this time, even when I made some bad choices. Likewise for my dad Lee, for all the sales lessons and countless meetings where we went to secure new business, and for the kindness he always showed me during his short time on this earth.

I have had the pleasure of working side by side with Stephen Fray in operations, logistics and brand development. Not only is he gifted and talented, but he knows the 3PL business like no one else. He can pick winning operations to do business with and knows how to work with and lead a winning team to victory, which leads to big dividends and rapid growth.

To Ray Anselmo, I'm very grateful for all his support and patience helping correct my spelling, which was atrocious at times ... well, most of the time. Ray always guided me in the right direction with kindness, not hurting my feelings along the way. We worked together for a short time at a 3PL warehouse at the beginning of our friendship—the experience there could be a whole other book! (We managed to cut it down to half a chapter for this one.) Thank you again for all of your help and support in the writing of this.

About the Author

Judy Jardine is a veteran of over thirty years in the logistics industry, working as a saleswoman and sales executive for warehousing, packaging and transportation. Currently she is a consultant and the founder of Truth About Logistics, a company that consults on third-party logistics concerns. She helps connect logistics companies with customers and other firms. She is also a frequent speaker at business and women's events.

Judy currently lives in Modesto, California.

If you need to improve your logistics business or find a logistics company to work with your product, contact Judy at truthaboutlogistics@gmail.com or call her at (209) 679-4975.

Judy can also be contacted on Linkedin, FaceBook, and Instagram at *judyloves99.

Contact Judy Jardine at truthaboutlogistics@gmail. to request a Free copy (How to Select A Warehouse) on a pdf $100.00 value absolutely Free.

www.ingramcontent.com/pod-product-compliance
Lightning Source LLC
Chambersburg PA
CBHW071420210326
41597CB00020B/3585